CIME DU GELAS   Italian side from NW

MERCANTOUR PARK
MARITIME ALPS

MOUNTAIN WALKING, TOURING AND CLIMBING

ROBIN G. COLLOMB

Rock climbs prepared by TONY MOULAM

West Col

MERCANTOUR PARK - MARITIME ALPS

First published 1985 by
West Col Productions
Goring   Reading   Berks. RG8 9AA

Copyright ©1985 West Col Productions

SBN 906227 26 7

Printed in England by Swindon Press Ltd
Swindon   Wilts.

Contents

Introduction	11
Background, Mercantour, Maritime Alps, Exploration, Access, Accommodation, hotels, huts, camping, Maps, Grading, Equipment, Scope of guide	
Valley Bases: Vésubie, Merveilles, Gesso	23
Huts and other mountain bases	25
Merveilles region – Mont Bego pre-historic engravings	37
Gordolasque – Roya divide	44
Clapier – Maledie frontier ridge	50
Frontier ridge: Gélas – St. Robert	59
Gordolasque – Fenestre divide	64
Boréon – Salèse basin	75
Lac Nègre basin	85
Argentera chain	95
High level touring routes	107
Selected technical rock climbs	110
Index	146

Illustrations

Peirabroc, Mt. Clapier, Chamineyes from Maledie	half title
Cime du Gélas from NW	frontis
Area map	8
Adus hut	31
Cougourde hut	31
Clapier – Maledie group	41
Gélas – St. Robert group	57
Cayre Colomb W side	65
Cayre Colomb E side	66
Grand Cayre – Ponset W side	68
Neiglier – Pointe André N side	71
Neiglier – Pointe André SW side	74
Cougourde from W	76
Tablasses – Préfouns group	88
Argentera group from SW	94
Argentera normal route schematic	97
Argentera W face	101
Argentera from SE	103
Ponset – Cayre Colomb E side	111
Ponset N face	112
Barel – Grand/Petit Cayres N side	114
Grand/Petit Cayres S side	117
Cougourde Peak 4 S face	123
Cougourde S and W/NW sides	124
Cayre des Erps	126
Cresta Savoia E side	131
Cima di Nasta W side	133
Madre di Dio ridge S side	135

Corno Stella S side	137
Guides' chain S side	142

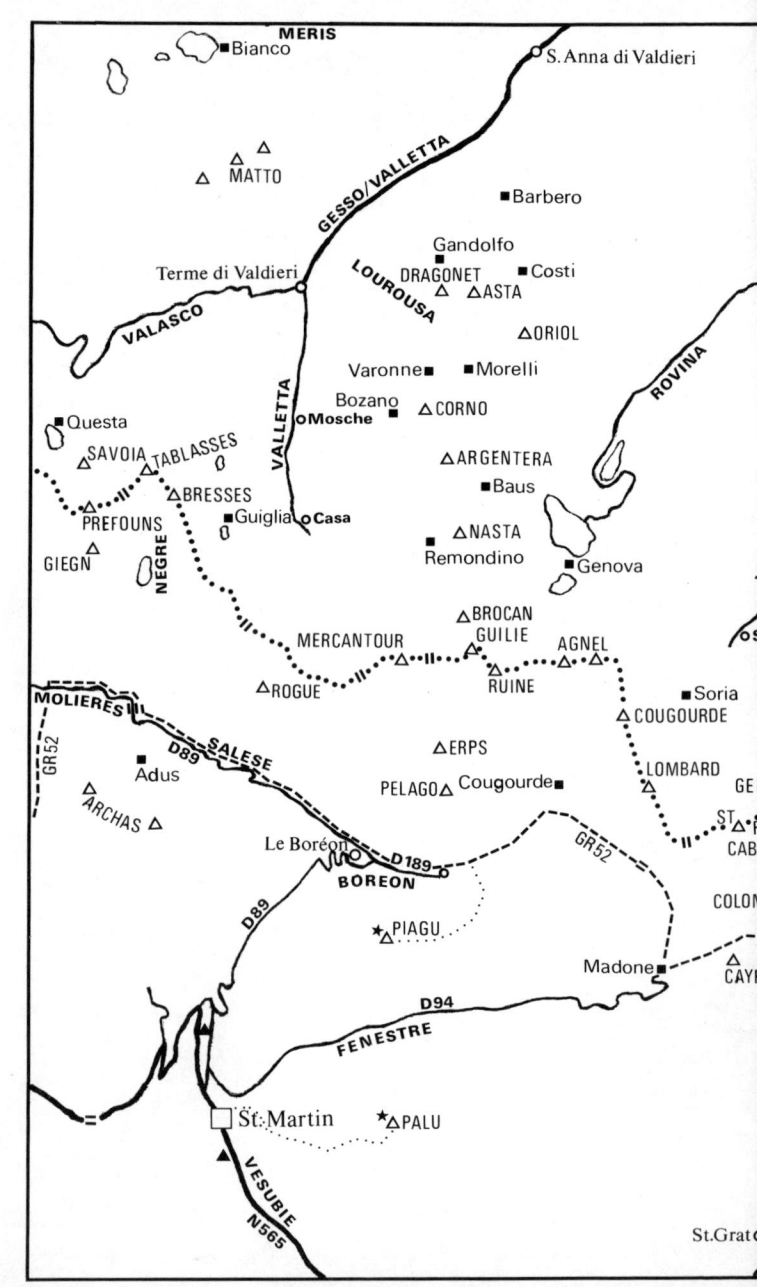

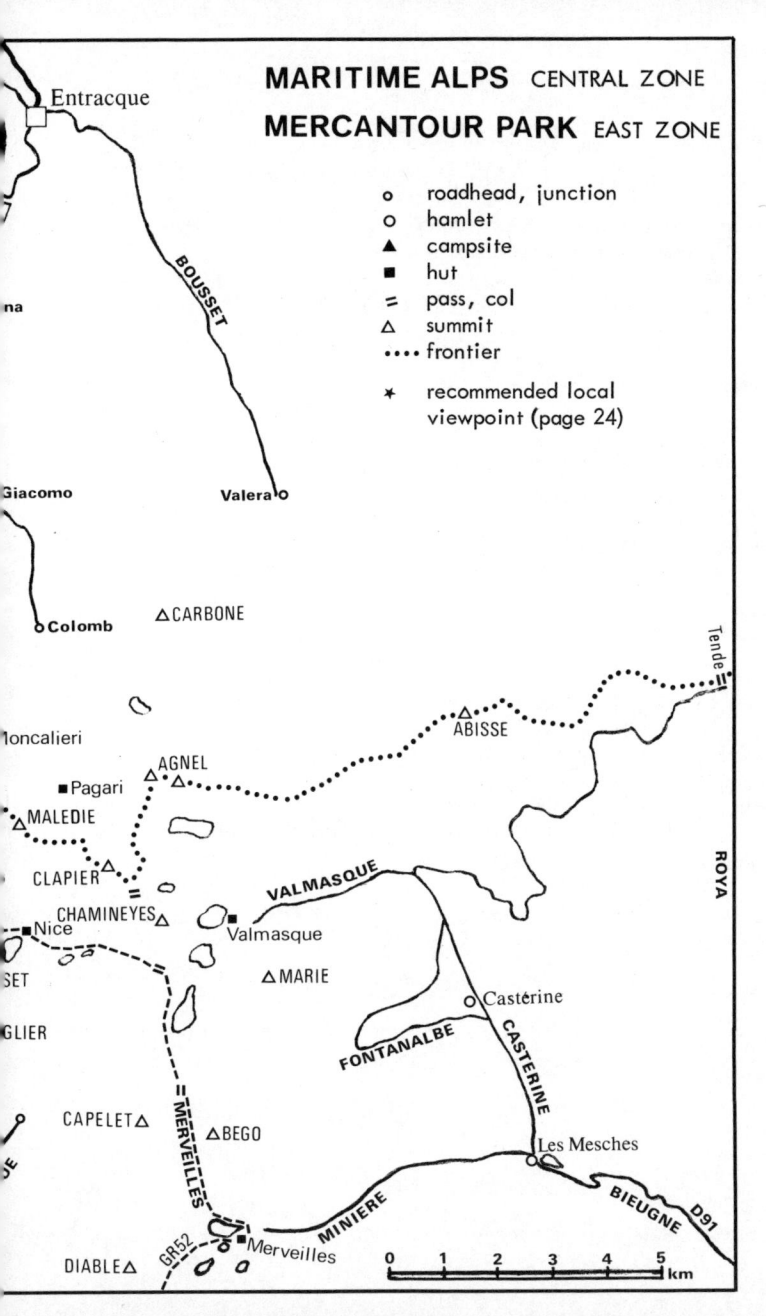

PUBLISHERS' NOTE

The original English guide to the Maritime Alps, published in 1968, contained a number of descriptions taken from Dr. Vincent Paschetta's definitive guide. These have now been revised in the light of work done by English field parties, notably in 1975 and 1978, while the most recent amendments from correspondents are included up to 1983. Photographs in the present work are by Robin Collomb and Tony Moulam and were taken in the month of September, though not in the same year.

ABBREVIATIONS

c.	approximately	L	left (direction)
CAF	French Alpine Club	m.	metres
CAI	Italian Alpine Club	min.	minutes
Fr.	French	mtn.	mountain
GM	Giovane Montagna	pt.	point, literally, or spot height
h.	hour(s)	R	right (direction)
Ital.	Italian	R.	route number cross reference
km.	kilometre(s)	rte.	route

N, S, E, W and intermediate directions, e.g. NW, SE

Baisse	saddle, col
Cayre (Caire)	pointed peak
Gias	chalet/pasture site
Pian	chalet/pasture site (implied on level ground)
Vacherie	cowshed(s)

Introduction

BACKGROUND

As long ago as 1960 Mercantour was proposed as a National Park but since then there has been a lot of controversy and little progress. Differences of opinion between developers, local people and the Conseil National de Protection de Nature (CNPN) emphasise the ambivalence of attitudes in France to the National Park concept. On one hand conservation is being preached whilst at the same time there is a desire to expand tourist facilities.

Until World War II Mercantour and the Ligurian Alps were protected from exploitation by developers by their geography which made it difficult to build approach roads; by the existence of the Italian Royal Hunting Reserve on both sides of the principal ridge and frontier system, and because their strategic role meant that the military could deny access to the public.

During the war and even after liberation chamois, ibex and other small game were massacred by soldiers with machine guns, and by the predatory poachers. Nevertheless when the idea of a game reserve was floated by the Conservateur des Eaux et Forêts it was supported by the hunters because they realised that the last few chamois were near to extinction. In 1953, 22,450 hectares were declared as the Reserve du Mercantour and wild life was protected for twenty years. Marmots, chamois and ibex re-established themselves, and mouflons (wild sheep) were introduced from Corsica. Eventually on 26 February, 1974 the area was made a 'Reserve National du Chasse' but this change did nothing to preserve beauty spots or to control building.

Since 1947, when the Italian part of Mercantour was returned to the French, civilisation has intruded its tentacles into the heart of the mountains in the form of roads penetrating valleys and water catchment schemes altering the configuration of formerly untouched areas of natural beauty. The main impetus was a great flood of tourists, which brought vandalism in its wake, even to the prehistoric engravings of the Merveilles valley. Another consequence of these hordes was the disappearance of unique flora and fauna.

Ski developments were suggested and in 1968 a special committee produced an inventory of possible locations. Mollières les Adus (Azur 2000), Sestrières, Chastillon (Isola 2000), Castérino-Caramagne and other places of lesser importance were all listed. A helicopter survey was carried out and the commission reported that "the valleys of the Basses-Alpes can be developed to provide a unique ski paradise". The report was circulated to the mayors of the eleven communes concerned and it galvanised the inhabitants into action as they envisaged a "white gold-rush" enlivening the poor villages which were dying of inertia and indolence.

Scientists and conservationists reacted vigorously and their concern was supported by public opinion. Despite this lobby many development schemes were planned discreetly and promoters worked clandestinely on the ground. The construction of Isola 2000 started in 1970 when a British promoter, financed by the Bernard Sunley Investment Trust, received sanction for a 6000 bed complex to be followed by accommodation for a further 5000, in a second phase. The commune was dispossessed of 2000 hectares of land and public money paid for the 18km. access road which was built. It cost 22 million francs and local taxes were doubled.

Isola 2000 was successfully opened but in a short time avalanches blocked the road for five weeks and the unhappy skiers had to be evacuated by helicopter. The phrase "isolated Isola" was coined. At the same time the local people realised that these enormous tourist havens were self supporting and that the mountain pillage to produce them provided no benefit to them.

The government was dismayed, announcing that "a check at Isola 2000 is serious because it implies that a great ski centre is not viable in the Maritime Alps" - exactly what the experts had predicted in 1971. They based their opinion on a formidable range of data, including statistics of the normal winter depth of snow and the minimum temperature, the length of winter, the slope profiles and not least the proximity of the Mediterranean - warm air increasing the risk of avalanches.

In spite of protests by CNPN and the Isola disaster entrepreneurs were not dissuaded. In August 1973 another road was built over the Col Mercière to link Isola 2000 with the Azur 2000 site. Other road developments allowed second home building to proliferate which, apart from disfiguring the landscape, put a heavy extra load on the relatively primitive local services.

To sum up, the conflict is between the desire for intense development to exploit tourism for the benefit of the local communities and the wish to retain for future generations the incomparable natural beauty of the land.

MERCANTOUR

The Mercantour massif has considerable interest because it lies between the Alps and the sea, being only 30 or 40 km. from the Mediterranean. With the advent of the bulldozer and similar modern ground equipment it is vulnerable to development as the radiating valleys provide access routes to the centre. The scenery is very varied with examples of Alpine meadows (Gordolasque, Castérine, Fontanalbe and Le Boréon); glacial lakes (Niré, Vens, Rabuons and Nègre, all above 2000m.) and the forests surrounding Mercantour where firs, spruce, larch, Arolla pines and Mugo pines abound. Above all the terrain from 2000m. to the peaks of 3000m. and more is often desolate with enormous blocks of rock chaotically tumbled about the ground and other places where Quaternary glaciers have smoothed out the contours. In fact small glaciers still exist on the N faces of the Gélas, Mt.Clapier and the Gd.Capelet. In the Merveilles valley there are prehistoric engravings dating from as long ago as the Mesolithic age, 3000 BC, to the fall of the Roman Empire. They are unique and without surveillance could well be destroyed or defaced by modern graffiti. The Alpine historian Coolidge was rarely wrong, but in 1880 he dismissed these "scribbles" as the work of idle shepherds, not realising how extensive they were.

Geological interest is typified by the dolomite and Karst limestone found in the Marguereis area where there are caves, gorges and subterranean rivers. On the Italian side of the Argentera the true Mercantour granite and gneiss are predominant and, in contrast, the Tinée and Var valleys are composed of sandstone, schist and various limestones.

One part of the region escaped Quaternary glaciation and this chance allowed a unique flora to survive. About 1500 species are present, 200 of them rated "rare". Entomologically Mercantour is the richest area in France, harbouring more endemic species than there are of plants. There is a diverse bird population and apart from ptarmigan, partridges, nutcrackers, dippers and Alpine accenters there are many owls. They include the Eagle owl, Tengmalm's owl and long and short-eared owls. The plight of mammals in the war has already been mentioned but the chamois is now firmly re-established. Ibex were brought into the Valdieri reserve about 1920 and the mouflon has flourished for 20 years. Unfortunately a shortage of wardens allows some poaching to go on.

The latest proposal for the National Park provides for extensions to the N and NW, to the edges of the Alpes-Maritimes department. It would include part of the Alpes du Haut Provence (le Lauzier, Cimet, Mt.Pelat and the Lac d'Allos) and the name Mercantour has thus been applied to an area much greater in size than that properly so called.

At the end of 1983 the locally published bulletin of the CAF in Nice, which comments frequently upon the machinations of internecine debate and inaction by officialdom, introduced its latest critique of these affairs with the words: The Mercantour National Park, created by legislation on 18 August, 1979, has hardly begun to make its presence felt during 5 years of existence - ardently supported and defended by some, violently opposed by others, progress towards achieving its aims creeps at a snail's pace. In 1984 an uproar was in progress about the state electricty board EDF's proposal to build a Rabuons barrage in the Tinée zone.

MARITIME ALPS

The Maritime Alps form the most southerly and westerly thrust of the Alpine chain in which the Mercantour zone is a constituent part. Taken as a whole the region is a large and dissected mountain range orientated NW - SE. Good walking and climbing can be found in all parts of the system but the main interest is concentrated in one area where the highest summits are located. This area lies due N of Nice. The frontier hereabouts runs W-E, and the S (Nice) side is approached directly by the Vésubie valley. The N (Italian) side is complicated by various valley approaches from Cuneo and the guidebook treats this side only with a summary, to give an indication of access to particular bases and mtn. huts. An adequate description of public services is also given.

The mountains described are collected in a small area which at first glance appears to be penetrated by a bewildering series of valleys. These valleys are quite long and small motor roads have now been made in most of them. Climbing in the district has been compared to that in the Isle of Skye but this is misleading. The most immediate impression of the climbing is that there is nothing freakish about it; it is much the same as in other parts of the Alps but there is often grass on the rocks, and sometimes lichen. Areas of clean rock are quite numerous, and the absence of snow climbs is only to be expected in a region where the maximum elevation is 3300m. and the average about 2900m.

While nearly all the peaks can be reached by walking routes, technical achievements in rock climbing have kept pace with standards found right across the Alps. The weather can be relied on as nowhere else in the Alps, although the mountains are often mist covered in the afternoon but clear during the evening.

Two notable features are the varied vegetation in the lower and middle valleys, which is sub-tropical, and the wilderness of stones and blocks that fills the upper valleys. The Mediterranean climate extends into the valleys, and between 750 and 1500m. there is a curious combination of Alpine and littoral vegetation. These valleys are breeding grounds for lizards and snakes. While reptiles are not usually considered a hazard by mountaineers, they have been seen above the snowline, even on the small glaciers, and climbers have pulled up on to a ledge to find a dozing viper.

The stony upper valleys can be reckoned among the roughest in the Alps. Vast areas of blocks, the size of houses, and masses of scree cover many slopes and sometimes the entire side of a mtn. This ground is known in the region as <u>clapier</u>. Paths, or the correct route over this terrain, are sometimes difficult to follow, and mountaineers with a flair for route finding have a definite advantage.

The rock is mainly gneiss with two or three important granite outcrops. Most of the rock is good, but there is always a lot of loose material on easy climbs, where the rock may also be poor. Some of the steep and unfrequented faces have brittle, flaky holds. Major rock routes on important ridges are usually furnished with obvious and easier variations, which avoid the challenge of keeping to the crest.

The N (Italian) side of the range is covered by a number of small but well formed glaciers, usually bare ice in mid-summer. The most appealing ice climb is the Canalone di Lourousa, some 900m. high on the NW side of the Argentera. Steep snow or ice slopes are found in gullies and on sheltered faces almost anywhere above 2700m. and they vary in extent from year to year. Stonefall is not a serious danger but care must be exercised to avoid dislodging stones when others are moving below. However, a more recent source of this hazard - possibly unique among the warnings to visitors anywhere in the Alps - arises from the large chamois herds now roaming freely in the Boréon-Salèse basin. These have become so tame that strings of animals will gallop quite closely past parties, dislodging a cannonade of stones. Several people caught unawares have been struck and injured in this way.

It is unusual to depart from a hut before daybreak, although there are a number of long approaches from bases in France to climb peaks on the frontier ridge, or in Italy, in one day. Early starts are advisable for expeditions such as the Argentera direct from Le Boréon and the Cresta Savoia from the Adus hut.

STORY OF EXPLORATION

Sardinian engineers made the earliest important ascents in the Maritime Alps; notably that of Mt.Clapier in 1818. Their greatly overestimated measurement of Cime Mercantour gave undue prominence to what was soon dismissed as a fairly insignificant hump situated roughly in the middle of the range. Revival of this long forgotten blunder is commemorated in the choice of name for the new Park zone. It was not until 1864 that Count Paolo di Saint-Robert brought mountaineering to the region with his ascent of the Gélas. The Niçois Jacques André visited the Madone in 1870 and probably climbed Mt.Ponset, Mt.Neiglier and two or three other summits. Then D.W.Freshfield arrived in 1878 and climbed the Nasta by mistake for the Argentera. In the following year W.A.B.Coolidge took advantage of this error and was the first to reach the highest point in the range by climbing the Lourousa couloir and traversing all four summits of the Argentera. The Coolidge party also climbed the Gélas and Mt.Clapier. Ludwig Purtscheller and the Günther brothers made new climbs on the Argentera in the 1890s. C.F.Meade visited the area in 1910 and made a good route on the Maledie.

Systematic exploration was started by the Niçois Victor de Cessole in 1898, although his colleague, Louis Maubert, had already climbed the Cime St.Robert, the Maledie and the Cougourde. Generally accompanied by the guides Jean Plent and Andréa Ghigo, De Cessole's list of first ascents is comparable (also in difficulty) with the Rydzewsky-Klucker list in the Bregaglia region of Switzerland. Virtually everything worth climbing by standards of the day - several hundred routes - was taken in their stride in the next 20 years. The notable Corno Stella bowed to this onslaught in 1903. De Cessole was the founder of the Nice section of the CAF.

The first series of modern routes was made by G. & J.Vernet and others between 1927 and 1935; a second series by K.Gurékian and others up to the wartime years. Throughout this period a constant champion of climbing in the Maritime Alps, Dr. Vincent Paschetta, dominated the scene.

On the Italian side of the range Bianco, Ellena and Soria were active for a period extending from 1927 to 1948; they are the true originators of the modern rock climb in this region, which is steep and serious and is approached with a no-nonsense attitude about artificial aids. Postwar climbing produced fleeting visits from people like Chabod and Terray, but the main contributions have been made by local climbers from Nice and Cuneo. Prominent activists in the 1950s and 1960s include F. & M.Dufranc and A.Gogna; F.Cravoisier, G.Demenge, E.Isch-Wall; F.Ruggeri and D.Ughetto, B & F.Salesi.

ACCESS

From Britain the best and most direct approach is to Nice, by road, rail or air. Fly/drive scheme between London and Nice, economical

for 3 or more persons. Flying time = 1¼ h. From Nice central bus sta,
behind E end of the Prom. des Anglais, bus service 5 times a day, up
and down, to St.Martin-Vésubie; less frequent before 1 July and after
15 September; 2 h., 65km. from Nice. Some buses call at airport. In
summer season, mini bus service St.Martin to Le Boréon (20 min.), St.
Martin to the Madone (40 min.), Roquebillière to Belvédère (15 min.).
Taxi hire at St.Martin and Roquebillière.

Parties wishing to travel directly to the Italian valleys should go to
Turin (rail and air services) and Cuneo (rail and coaches from Turin).
Fly/drive scheme from London to Turin. From Cuneo (90km. from
Turin) bus service two or three times daily in summer to Terme di Valdieri (Matto-Argentera) and Entracque (Argentera, Gélas, Clapier),
1 h. New roads from both centres penetrate towards the frontier ridge
and service hydro-electric projects. The road in the Rovina valley
was still closed to the public recently; permission to use it can be
obtained from the local supervisor at Piastra above Entracque.

ACCOMMODATION, HOTELS, HUTS, CAMPING

Hotels and pensions at St.Martin are numerous and cover a wide
price range. Modest pockets are catered for in surprisingly large
hotels. Visitors are advised to consult the helpful tourist office situated in a corner of the main market square. There are a few hotels at Le
Boréon, Roquebillière and Belvédère. Camping at St.Martin is restrict-
ed by agricultural and forestry commitments and a list of sites available
to N and S of village will be provided by the tourist office. Camping
at the Madone and Le Boréon is unofficial (no site services) but is
widely practised. You are advised to get permission first and secure
if possible an authorisation written on tourist office notepaper. While
the local commune is divided and resisting formalisation of the Park
straightforward camping arrangements are unlikely to emerge. Simple
mtn. camping in the upper valleys, where the terrain permits, can be
freely carried out.

Huts on the French side of the Maritime Alps have been much improved during the 1970s. The main ones have wardens and a restaurant
service in summer, with self catering facilities in some of them. Huts
without wardens are closed and locked. These are fully equipped and
only food and a small stove need be taken. Apply to the St.Martin
tourist office for address of the key holder; in the late 1970s this was
the area forestry warden, in a side street near centre of the village;
he will produce all keys required, normally against a deposit which
will be waived if you have a current continental alpine club member-
ship card. You pay on returning the keys. Hut rates, with a lower
scale of charges for closed huts, are among the cheapest in the Alps.
Night rate in 1984, F.Fr. 36;(with reciprocal rights, 18).

A few Italian huts have wardens but most of them are closed and locked. Keys are no longer kept in St.Martin. Parties crossing the border in summer to stay in Italian huts have an even chance of finding premises open and occupied, when payment can be made in hut boxes provided. Be warned however that parties have gone into Italy and have found huts locked and unoccupied. Keys are kept at Terme di Valdieri, S. Anna di Valdieri and Entracque, generally in hotels or with a local farmer. The situation in which the French no longer have an arrangement to supply keys for Italian huts (except from the CAF office in Nice) has largely arisen because of road construction leading in some cases to within 1 h. or less walking distance from previously quite remote hut sites. Ordinary tourists with cars could therefore visit and use huts if the doors were left open by authorised mtn. parties. Restricting the latter to authorisation from the Italian side effects a degree of control over the situation.

MAPS

Several important changes in maps available have occurred in the 1970s. The choice and thereby confusion have widened. It only remains to be said that this guide is based entirely on details found in the 1977 tourist edition of the 1/25,000 (25m.) IGN map, though now out of print. All mapping is of a high standard, multi-coloured and accurately contoured.

<u>IGN maps</u> (French national survey)

Statutory grid sheets:

100m. R-20 Viève   R-21 Nice (better quality than no.61)

50m. 3740 Le Boréon   3741 St.Martin-Vésubie

25m. Le Boréon 5-6   Le Boréon 7-8   Will probably be phased
St.Martin-Vésubie 1-2 and 3-4   out in the 1980s

Tourist sheets:

100m. 61 Nice-Barcelonnette (with overprinted information, covers a wide area beyond mtn. zone)

25m. 258 Haute Vésubie   259 Haute Roya (both with overprints)
These maps were withdrawn in 1982/3, owing to objections to the amount of Italian ground shown, including all the Argentera massif. They have been replaced by two new 25m. sheets double the size of 25m. statutory sheets, but cut back severely so that the Italian terrain is omitted. For the present the DR and IGC maps must be used for this ground. The new 25m. sheets are:

3741 Ouest St.Martin-Vésubie (covers most of guidebook area)
3841 Ouest Merveilles-Roya
both maps have overprinted tourist information

DR/IGN map

50m. 9 Haut-Pays Niçois (covers wide surrounding area)

IGC map

50m. 8 Alpi Marittime e Liguri (similar to DR map but more orientated to Italian side of range)

Paschetta maps

50m. The key Vésubie sheet in this series of 3 maps has now been out of print for nearly 20 years and is sought after as a collector's item. Of its kind it has never been bettered. The Tinée-Haut Var sheet (not part of this guidebook area) may still be available locally.

Warning: The accuracy/position of paths and some topographic detail is clearly doubtful on all maps where the Italian side of the range is shown. For instance, approaches to the Remondino and Questa huts are imperfectly indicated; indeed annoying little errors can be found for all huts situated in Italy.

IGN, DR and IGC maps are available from West Col Productions.

GUIDEBOOKS

A large number of French and Italian guidebooks are published for the Maritime Alps, both for walking and climbing. They are not generally available in Britain.

ALTITUDES, NOMENCLATURE, LANGUAGE

All heights and topographical references are taken from the 1977 IGN 25m. tourist map. Spellings on this map may differ in some respects from traditional spellings, and further changes have been introduced in the 1983 25m. map. Other variations in names used are sometimes included for interest. Place names in the Maritime Alps have interesting meanings and an explanation of them is given in the appropriate route descriptions. French is spoken on both sides of the frontier, and Italian is generally understood in the French villages. English and German are rarely heard.

GRADING OF ROUTES AND CLIMBS

Only rock climbing grades of I to VII in roman numerals are used in this guide, qualified for more accuracy by minus (-) and plus (+) signs; thus II-, II, II+ is the rising order through grade II. As applied to the Maritime Alps, the lower stages of this system equate to:

- I- Easy walking along a footpath, possibly steep and rocky in parts.
- I   Walking up steep narrow rocky tracks, crossing steep trackless and rough terrain with short bits of rock scrambling.
- I+ As above but always trackless, with steep loose terrain, easy but exposed rock pitches, moderately inclined snow slopes.
- II- Fairly continuous rock scrambling with short pitches for which a rope is advised; steep snow slopes.
- II Moderately difficult rock pitches, rope required; snow/ice slopes.
- II+ Rock climbing with some technical difficulty. Snow/ice slopes requiring step cutting or crampons. Equates to "Difficult" in British rock climbing parlance.
- III/VII Normal alpine scale interpretation.

EQUIPMENT

Snow and ice climbing equipment need not be taken on the majority of expeditions. Descriptions indicate where an axe or crampons might be useful. Rock climbing equipment is not indicated in detail and experienced alpinists will be able to determine gear requirements from the assessments accorded to routes described.

SCOPE OF GUIDE

The guidebook is designed to cater both for mtn. walking and touring parties as well as climbers. For the latter, some routes in the highest grades are mentioned only as notes. As a general rule mtn. walking parties should not embark on routes graded higher than II-, and at this level they should be experienced in serious rock scrambling and route finding. Waymarks and artificially equipped trails are mainly absent in the Maritime Alps - the exact opposite, for instance, to the Julian Alps and the Dolomites. Though distances could be shorter and route times less, the terrain is more complicated than anything that might be found in these two areas.

Valley bases

VÉSUBIE

Main road along Nice sea front (Prom. des Anglais) now has parallel seaward side motorway access lane in Cannes (W) direction. Interchange junction near Nice airport at entrance to Var valley, RN 202. It is better to follow the old road alongside railway to within 2 km. of the congested Var junction where a secondary road forks R to enter RN 202 above (N of) the motorway junction. The RN 202 is a fast flat road followed for 25 km. to the Plan du Var; one-way traffic junctions on R (E) to enter Vésubie valley, N 565. The fairly narrow N 565 with excellent road surface twists up the deep rocky Vésubie gorge with numerous blind bends and short tunnels, to villages of St. Jean la Rivière, Lantosque and Roquebillière.

Roquebillière, old village on main road (596m.), new village on hillside to W (610m.). Junction on R (E) to Belvédère (837m.) at the entrance to Gordolasque valley. All main services, hotels, etc.

Valley road continues without incident to St. Martin, bus sta. on L side of final uphill stretch to central market place; 64 km. from Nice.

St. Martin-Vésubie (964m.), a large village built at head of the Vésubie where the valley divides to become the Boréon (N) and the Fenestre (E). All main services, about 25 hotels and pensions, tourist office in market place, guides' bureau; main shopping centre, varied and comprehensive, in old main street adjoining marketplace. This narrow cobbled thoroughfare has the former sewer drain down its centre and is closed to vehicles except for goods access. Walking route to the Madone goes out from top of this street.

From marketplace continue by main road (passing inconspicuous turning on R for the Madone road) up the Boréon valley, crossing and recrossing the river (junction on L to Valdeblore-St. Dalmas), to reach a final section in zigzags ascending to Le Boréon hamlet (1473m.) beside a small barrage. Two hotels, one inn, generally closed after 15 September. The good road surface ends at a fork with parking places; L for Salèse valley (bunkhouse a short way up here on R), R for the upper Boréon valley; 8 km. from St. Martin, mini-bus service in summer.

MERVEILLES

An outline description of this area, famous for its prehistoric carvings, is given in a later section of the guide; several easy summits and rock scrambling of interest in same area. Direct access from St. Dalmas-de-Tende on the main Nice - Col de Tende road by small roads and jeep lanes. Bus and jeep hire services, highly organised for trippers in summer. Walking routes from St. Martin neighbourhood are noted in the same section.

GESSO VALLEY

This valley runs SW from Cuneo (Coni) (537m.) into the heart of the Italian side of the Maritime Alps. Main road N 20 to Borgo San Dalmazzo (641m.), where it continues S over the Col de Tende to Nice. After junction on this road, continue by good smaller road to Valdieri (774m., 18km.) and in a further 2km. reach side road to L (S) leading to Entracque (904m.) in another 4 km. (24km. from Cuneo, 136km. from Nice across Col de Tende). Bus service three times a day during summer. Hotels, shops, restaurants, etc. Three rough continuation roads lead into the high valleys towards the frontier ridge.

Passing the junction to Entracque, the valley road continues good to S. Anna di Valdieri (1011m.), a hamlet (two inns, etc.), after which the road narrows and climbs steadily to the isolated hamlet of Terme di Valdieri (1368m.) where the Gesso valley divides and is towered over either side by Mte. Matto and the Argentera (15 km. from Valdieri, 33 km. from Cuneo, 145 km. from Nice across Col de Tende). Bus service twice daily. Large termal baths hotel, one good inn with a restaurant, small pension/restaurant, small shop. Two important rough continuation roads pass into the upper valleys.

Scenic viewpoints

Two especially recommended viewpoints for a day trip above St. Martin and the Vacherie du Boréon carpark (R.11), clearly marked on map:

1) Cime de la Palu (2132m.), waymarked path from the St. Antoine br. (973m.) on E side of St. Martin, $3\frac{1}{2}$ h. in ascent, $1\frac{1}{2}$ h. for descent.

2) Cime de Piagu (2338m.). A short way along R.11 beyond the Boréon carpark, signpost on R (S) for the Mairis pass. Continue along ridge W to summit, 2 h. in ascent, 1 h. for descent.

Huts and other mountain bases

Note: Huts and summits in the Merveilles region and outline information about the famous rock engravings are dealt with briefly in the next section of the guide. These include the huts of the Merveilles, Valmasque; the summits of Mt. Bego, Diable, Capelet, Chaminèye and their passes.

Nice   2232m.

CAF. Situated at the bottom of the SW spur of Mt. Clapier, and a short distance above the NE end of the small barrage lake now flooding the Fous plain, right at the top of the Gordolasque valley. The old hut is still intact but normally locked, a few m. higher on a knoll, for use out of season and in winter; entrance through rear loft door; keys at St. Martin. Main hut has a warden and staff, restaurant service 1 June to 30 Sept., separate self-cooking room. Places for 80 in dormitories. Good campsites near hut, water plentiful.

1. By the Gordolasque valley, the shortest and most direct route if one has transport to roadhead. I-.

Reach Belvédère village in entrance to Gordolasque valley by bus or car. The sharp turning up the valley road is $\frac{1}{2}$km. below village centre at pt. 829m. Drive narrow metalled road up valley through St. Grat hamlet (hotels) at a moderate gradient for about 18 km. to large carparking area at top (1800m.). Taxi hire easy.

Follow continuation footpath mostly over fairly steep stony ground and rock outcrops to N, soon passing small fork R to Lac Autier, then zigzagging above the Estrech waterfall to enter a large shallow grassy gully which emerges in a trough at top, under pt. 2022m. Cross stones trending L, old waymarks; do not bear straightahead. Cross stream to its L side and join original footpath coming up L side of stream/valley. The path continues mounting steadily away from the stream over grass and rocks, easing off to contour into the small Barme plain (2136m.). Excavations here have destroyed original path; a small track with a few waymarks keeps L of terraced earthworks and shortly reaches junction L to the Madone. Continue near the stream up to barrage wall ahead. Ascend a small track L across two jeep road levels running R (2173m.), aiming to follow L (W) shore of lake, waymarks. Follow jeep road along lakeside to an obvious and slightly higher path starting where the jeep road drops towards the water's edge. Follow this path over scree and rocks, contouring round N end of lake to marshy, grassy ground to join by moving E a better path rising in a few short zigzags R to hut.

2 h. from carpark roadhead.

2. From the Madone (1903m.) over the Pas du Mont Colomb (2548m.). Probably the most classic mtn. walking pass in the region. As many parties visit the Nice hut by this approach as from the Gordolasque valley. A stage on the Mercantour high level route and part of GR52. Until early July a fairly steep snow slope rests on the Madone side, so ice axe advisable. I-/I.

From the Madone (roadhead ex. St.Martin, R.8) follow path past the church on its R side and descend to the stream, crossed by a bridge. Go N along R side of stream above a little gorge, then ascend E over grassy slopes and rocks on a small track below the Cayre de la Madone. Higher up, work more to R towards smooth rockbanks forming an obvious little barrier covered with black lichen; skirt the foot of it. Reach a spur from where a grassy plain (Gias Cabret) in the stream bed can be seen. Head up R towards the Cayre, to below its rocks, then make a rising traverse over large scree at the foot of the N gully of the Baisse du Cayre. So reach the entrance to the valley proper below the pass (1 h.). Ascend the valley below the N face of Mt.Ponset, along the grass terraces on L side of bed, then in the bed, up to the Lac du Mt. Colomb (2390m.). The pass lies due E. Climb scree and snow with a small track to top and turn a sharp pinnacle in gap on the R (S) side (2 h. from Madone, $1\frac{1}{2}$ h. in descent).

On the other (Gordolasque) side descend a short gully then a small track in fairly steep scree to grass, and continue down keeping to L side of the shallow valley trough; ignore tracks going off L. Near the bottom follow a large footpath in a few zigzags to junction with R.1 at N end of the Barme plain. Follow R.1 to Nice hut ($1\frac{1}{4}$ h. from pass to hut, $3\frac{1}{4}$ h. from Madone. Same time in reverse direction).

3. From the Merveilles hut (2111m.) over the Baisse de Valmasque (2549m.) and Baisse du Basto (2693m.). A much frequented stage of the GR52. One of the most interesting hut connections in the park, going past the much visited and most important of the Merveilles rock engravings. These are described in next section of the guide. Route finding needs care - in cloud, quite tricky; small discontinuous track on both sides of the Basto saddle. Steep snow patches possible in early season. Confusing nomenclature on some older maps. I-/I.

From the Merveilles hut (R.25) follow the main path W above S side of Lac Long Sup. After a junction L (ignore) it swings N into the basin entrance of the Merveilles valley to reach beside the stream a junction of paths. Either cross stream to R (E) side and follow up near the bed from where rock carvings sites may be visited; large asterisk indicators mark approaches to carvings. Or remain on L (W) side and wind up and across rockbanks below another series of carvings. Both ways lead to just beyond a small lake where the paths unite (2294m.). Continue up R side of stream past two tarns (2383m.) to a series of zigzags mounting comfortably to the saddle of the Baisse de Valmasque (1½ h.)

On the other (N) side descend scree or snow in a few zigzags to a prominent junction where the slope eases. Take the L (NW) branch in a rising traverse over a huge terrace below the Têtes du Basto and above the large Basto lake. The track is fairly clear up to a tarn which is passed in its L (W) side, then it works up a shallow rocky valley in the same direction towards the enclosing ridge at the top. Ignore the lowest ridge gap to L, under the Basto rocks, and aim for a shoulder in the ridge a little to the R of the first ridge hump above the lowest gap. Go up grassy rocks and scree direct (N) to this shoulder, the Baisse du Basto (1 h.).

On the other (W) side go straight down steep grass into a series of broken gullies with stones and grass in their beds to a rib and broken ground below. This section might have snow cover until mid-July. A small track zigzags down L side of rib below the shapely Cayre Autier (2676m.), to reach a little plateau (2493m.). Continue straight down (W) to the upper Lac Niré (2379m.); cross the ground between the middle and upper pools to a junction on N side. Turn L (W) and follow small track past the middle pools to the main lake (2351m.). The little track goes down grassy bluffs then slants L across the lake outfall to a bluff overlooking the Fous valley stream. Descend sharp R (away from hut direction) and cross the Fous stream in a little grassy plain (2240m.). Turn L (W) and follow a grassy track above stream gorge, keeping R and ascending a little to turn a rocky hillock by a grassy trough dividing the hillock from the great spur of Mt.Clapier above. Descend from the trough bearing a little L to reach Nice hut (1 h., 3½ h. from Merveilles hut, same time in reverse direction).

4. From the Valmasque hut across the Pas de la Fous (2828m.). A stage on the classic high level route. Similar terrain to the more direct GR52 section which avoids the Valmasque hut by crossing the Baisse du Basto (R.3). Track vague in places and difficult to find, but careful route finding avoids complications. Normally snow patches to mid-July or later. I-/I.

From Valmasque hut (2221m.) cross the dam wall of Lac Vert to S and slant up slabby rockbands S to join the old mule trail near pt.2294m. Continue by this trail to Lac Noir (2278m.) and cross its dam wall W. A small track goes W up grassy slopes above, directly towards the Pas du Chaminèye (a more direct and steeper route to the Nice hut). In 5 min. reach a track running R (N then NW). Follow this in a rising traverse under Cime Lusière, in a shallow, narrow trough up to a little plateau where the Lac de la Lusière (2625m.) is found. This tarn nestles in a hollow above the larger Gelé lake (2588m.). The Fous pass lies immediately above and W of the tarn. Ascend direct over grass on a small track into the little cwm below the pass. Keep to the R (N) side of cwm

where the track makes the best use of grass, finally reaching the top by
a short traverse L (2 h.). A worthwhile diversion of 20 min. is to ascend
rubble slopes of Cime Viglino (2910m.) to N (R.49). Excellent views
of Mt. Clapier, Maledie and their N face glaciers.

On the other (W) side, do not descend direct. Make a slightly descending traverse, keeping fairly high and R, heading due W towards the
rocks flanking the SE ridge of Mt. Clapier. Cross a rib in the upper cwm
and below the Clapier rocks descend the R side of the upper Fous cwm
over scree, stones and large blocks. Keeping away from the immediate
flanking scree slopes under Mt.Clapier, there are grassy strips in this
ground somewhat L, linked by a few cairns. About 15 min. after leaving the pass, bear more to R again and descend rocks and large blocks
(vague track) round the N end of the Fous rock barrier, concealed
below, which closes the middle valley. Below the level of the barrier
trend L (SW) again and go down grassy steps to a little grassy plain at
2367m. under the central barrier. Sheepfold. Now follow down the
R side of the Fous stream, various small/vague tracks in grass, and
after 15 min. trend away from the stream and go up a little to cross a
grassy trough between a rocky hillock L and the SW spur of Mt.Clapier
on R. Beyond trough descend keeping L a little to hut (1h., $1\frac{3}{4}$ h. in
ascent to pass; 3 h. from Valmasque hut, $3\frac{1}{4}$ h.in reverse direction).

Pagari (Federico Federici)   2650m.

5. CAI. A pendant to the Nice hut, on Ital. side of the frontier and
below the Pas de Pagari, between Mt. Clapier and the Maledie and at
the edge of the small Pagari glacier. Easily reached across this pass
(R.57) in $2\frac{1}{2}$ h. From the rough roadhead just below the Gias Colomb
(1444m.), above San Giacomo d'Entracque, by waymarked footpath
M13 in 4 h. Fully equipped with butane cooker, etc., places for 30,
door normally locked, keys at S.Giacomo (inn), Entracque and at the
CAF H.Q. in Nice.

Moncalieri/Lago Bianco   2553m.

6. GM. Situated on the NE side of Lago Bianco (2549m.), in a
glacier cwm below the N (Ital.) side of Cime Chafrion, between the
Gélas and Maledie. Opened in 1972, butane cooking, etc., places
for 40. Door locked, keys at San Giacomo d'Entracque. From rough
roadhead just below the Gias Colomb (1444m.), partly by R.5 along
waymarked trail M13 towards the Pagari hut for one km., then up a
steep track, not always continuous, into the Lago Bianco cwm. Red
waymarks ($3\frac{1}{4}$ h.from roadhead). Inter-connection between Pagari
and Moncalieri huts over Passo soprano del Muraion (2430m.) in $1\frac{1}{2}$ h,
either direction.

Dado Soria   1840m.

7.   CAI. Situated on the Ital. side of the Col de Fenestre, on a spur above the mule trail, to its E, in a section of the valley called the Praiet which is linked through the Pierastretta gorge to the main Gesso della Barra valley below. The hut faces the 'rear' or E side of the Cougourde. Above Entracque cars can be driven to San Giacomo in 9 km. (1213m.) where the valley divides. In the R branch a rough road is suitable for small cars and jeeps up to parking at 1450m. near the Siula huts, 4 km. from S. Giacomo. This is waymarked trail M11 to the Col de Fenestre. Then about $1\frac{1}{4}$ h. walking from roadhead along R side of the Pierastretta gorge, or $2\frac{1}{4}$ h. all the way on foot from S. Giacomo. Fully equipped and comfortable with gas cooking and lighting, places for 35, door locked, keys at S. Giacomo (inn) and Entracque.

Madone de Fenestre   1903m.

8.   CAF. Easily the most frequented hut site in the region, situated at roadhead in the Fenestre valley, 11 km. from St. Martin. Long car parking area below the Madone buildings. Mini bus and taxi services from St. Martin. On foot, use road for half the distance; where this crosses to R (S) side of valley for first time (c.1500m.) continue ahead by the original mule path on L side, 3 h. Unauthorised camping on excellent sites near stream below Madone buildings (to E). The CAF premises are on L (N) side of terrace between the buildings as one approaches church at back of terrace. Restaurant service, no self-catering permitted, warden and staff from 15 June to 30 October. Places for 62 in rooms and dormitory. Out of season room with places for 20, normally locked, keys at St. Martin. Traverse from Nice hut, reverse R.2.

9.   From the Cougourde hut across the Pas des Ladres (2448m.). Part of the classic high level route and a section of GR52. A fine ramble, mostly good track, snowfield on the Boréon side until late July, much frequented. I-.

From Cougourde hut (2090m.) descend E from the terrace to the main stream, plank bridge, and join a little track going SSE down L side, yellow triangles, in open forest. In a few min. cross outfall from the Gaisses cwm above (E) and reach a little fork. Keep L and traverse almost horizontally to a large overhanging rock, followed by a descending traverse over large blocks, levelling out to cross another zone of trees before reaching the main Pas des Ladres footpath coming up from the Peirastrèche chalet (1936m.) in the Boréon valley. Go up a little rocky defile (2187m.) and emerge on the N side of the Lac de Trecolpas (Tre Coulpas) (2150m.). Continue up the valley SE to the steeper headslopes. The first section may be snow covered and fairly steep, otherwise a good zigzag track, followed by an upper section on scree to the saddle ($1\frac{3}{4}$ h.). At the saddle there is a high level track going L (E) to the Col de Fenestre; ignore.

On the other (Fenestre) side descend a zigzag track in the middle of a little cwm, passing another L fork traverse track as one emerges from the cwm. Cross broad grass slopes still in the same direction and reach the lower section of the Col de Fenestre mule trail by a series of sharp zigzags beside the Rostagn stream. Continue down large trail to the Madone (1 h., $2\frac{3}{4}$ h. from Cougourde hut, same time in reverse).

10. From St. Grat hamlet, hotels (1547m.) in the Gordolasque valley (road access from Belvédère), by a good footpath to the Col de Prals (2335m.) (2 h.). On the Fenestre side a path descends the Prals valley to the Madone road not far from the Madone itself ($1\frac{1}{2}$ h., $3\frac{1}{2}$ h. in all. $3\frac{1}{4}$ h. in reverse direction). Clearly shown on map. I-.

Cougourde 2090m.

CAF. Single storey prefabricated hut on a terrace above the stream almost at the top of the upper Boréon valley. Warden and simple restaurant service 1 July to 30 September, places for 35. Out of season, keys at St.Martin. Self catering inconvenient. Warden will prepare food brought up by visitors. Good campsites nearby, sheltered, water plentiful. Traverse from Madone hut, reverse R.9.

11. From Le Boréon hamlet (1473m.), bus and taxi services from St. Martin. The tarmac road continues E for nearly one km. to a junction at a bend, carparking. Bear R along a broad unmade road going up the Boréon valley, easy for cars, and continue for 3 km. to large carpark and picnic area near the Vacherie du Boréon (1690m.). Taxi hire from St.Martin, easy. From Le Boréon bus terminus on foot, 1 h. Signpost at back of carpark. Follow a broad level forest trail E and eventually pass a small weir beside the stream, leading to a zigzag section in rocks, then a section in open forest level again to cross stream to L side by a bridge (1838m.). Continue pleasantly near stream with picturesque large blocks scattered round and so reach the little triangular cow dung plain of the Peirastrèche chalet (1936m.). Signpost at far N side. Ascend trending L quite steeply with a few waymarks to the top of a rocky bluff. Alternatively, go R to beside a bridge over the stream giving access R to the Pas des Ladres path. Stay on L side for a few paces then ascend a rocky path to top of bluff. Continue along grassy terraces and over rocks above the stream gorge into open forest; the path rises steadily to hut platform ($1\frac{1}{2}$ h. from carpark roadhead, $2\frac{3}{4}$ h. from Le Boréon hamlet on foot). I-.

Above: ADUS HUT
COUGOURDE HUT

Adus   2163m.

CAF. Adous on map. Situated on an idyllic pasture, glades and trees, above the S side of the Salèse valley. As a base for climbs in the Préfouns group a descent and reascent of 200m. across the Col de Salèse is involved with all excursions. Firewood stove, fully equipped, places for 12-15. Water from small stream in forest 100m. distance to SW. Door locked, keys at St.Martin.

12.   From Le Boréon hamlet (1473m.), bus and taxi services from St. Martin. The tarmac road continues E for nearly one km. to a junction at a bend, carparking. Take L branch (to NW) for the Col de Salèse. The road up the Salèse valley in the 1970s was still very rough though passable for cars. It is never narrow but reaches 1 in 6 gradients on some bends. Surfacing the road is long overdue but adverse economic priorities have prevailed. Frequently traversed to date by all kinds of cars and easy for jeeps. Expensive taxi ride. From Le Boréon to Col de Salèse (2031m.) , 7 km. (Road surface on the W or Tinée side of pass is better and at an easier angle). On foot, Le Boréon - Col de Salèse, starting up a shortcut footpath to avoid the initial loop to E, 2 h. A direct track from the road at pt. 1807m. in the forest to hut is a stiff walk but saves at least 30 min. for those without transport.

At the Col de Salèse, carparking on wide verges. Precisely at top, a track mounts due W along a wooded rib, narrow in places, and curves round S to enter a little hollow which is crossed to a few zigzags in rocks and trees, followed by a contouring movement L and short descents to a grassy hollow beside forest. Ascend to a hillock (2232m.) then descend SE over a fine pasture to hut (45 min. from col, 30 min. in descent). I-.

Genova   old site, 1914m.   new site, 2020m.

13.   CAI. At top of the Valle della Rovina, a branch above Entracque, new barrage construction in 1974 has flooded old site. New site is found above the SW shore of the lake (Lago del Chiotàs, 1978m.), between this artificial lake and Lago Brocan (2000m.) further S. New jeep road constructed round both sides of the Chiotàs basin, with direct access up the Rovina valley contractors' road, closed at present to private cars but permission can be obtained from the Paistra barrage near Entracque. 7 km. of road from Ponte della Rovina. From barrage roadhead at the Chiotàs dam wall to new hut, 30 min. on foot. Gas cooking, etc., 30 places, door locked, keys at Entracque. From the Cougourde hut, over the Col de la Ruine (2724m.) in $3\frac{1}{2}$ h.

Baus Bivouac   2676m.

14.   CAI.   Situated below the terminal pyramid of the SE spur of the Argentera. A rough wooden shelter with room for 5. No facilities and probably in poor condition. Access, formally from the old Genova hut, has been altered by the new barrage of the Lago del Chiotàs (see R.13).

Morelli   2450m.

15.   CAI.   Rif. Costanzo Morelli e Alvaro Buzzi. Situated in the Lourousa valley, SE of Terme di Valdieri. By waymarked path N8, $3\frac{1}{4}$ h. Fully equipped, gas cooking and lighting, places for 54. Door locked, keys at Gaina farm on road between Terme and Sant'Anna di Valdieri.

Terme di Valdieri biv. huts

16.   CAI.   There are two biv. huts in the Asta Soprana-Sottana-Dragonet group of rock peaks, N of the Morelli hut, which serve good technical climbing in this group above the Gesso valley road. Nicolino Gandolfo (1847m.) and Roberto Barbero (1670m.), marked with reasonable precision on IGC map. A third, Mauro Costi (2275m.), has now been constructed.

Silvio Varrone Bivouac   old hut, 2100m.   new hut, c.1950m.

17.   CAI.   Situated almost directly below the Lourousa (NW) couloir of the Argentera, approached up the Lourousa valley as for R.15, then by a branch track, N9, to S, $2\frac{3}{4}$ h. from Terme di Valdieri. A tiny shelter below overhanging rock, 4 places but has gas cooking. A new shelter was built in 1975 on L (E) side of small track to site, about 150m. below old shelter. Places for 10, most of the material comforts removed from old shelter to new. New red waymarks. Keys at Gaina farm, as for R.15.

Franco Remondino   2430m.

CAI. An important hut site on a small promontory in the Assedras cwm below the W face of the Cima di Nasta; a stage on approaching the easiest routes for climbing the Argentera, and for access from France to the best climbs in the Argentera-Corno Stella group. Rebuilt in 1968, warden at weekends in summer, simple restaurant service, places for 55 in rooms and dormitory. Keys at Gaina farm on main road in Gesso valley between Terme and Sant'Anna di Valdieri.

18.   From Terme di Valdieri rough road in the Valletta valley is motorable to Pian della Casa (1743m.), but it is better to leave cars at the Gias della Casa (1678m.), $1\frac{3}{4}$ h. on foot. From here to roadhead, one

km., parking possible, then after another very rough 200m. to signpost on L (E), waymarked path N11, in zigzags towards the Madre di Dio then traversing into the Assedras valley; keep L at a junction and so recross streams (path N12 to R). Continue fairly steeply above the L side of stream to cross it higher up and ascend a gully to reach the hut further R (2 h. from Casa chalets). I-. Lower section of path line on all maps situated too far N.

19. From Le Boréon hamlet over the Col de Guilié (2650m.), a committing walk in remote country, large snowfields possible on the Italian side. Ice axe essential. I-/I. (Col Guilié, 2639m. on IGN 25m. map). A proposal exists to build a hut in the Guilié cwm; if this materialises it will have a profound bearing on the length of the excursions begun by R.19.

From Le Boréon bus terminus follow road along barrage lake to the Cavallé inn on L, just before end of lake. On R side of inn take a path curving R past chalets to join the Col de Salèse road. Go down this for a few paces to a vehicle access track to bunkhouse and waymarked path (signpost) rising L (N) above road. Follow this over pasture past chalets to edge of the forest, small crossroads (1588m.). Continue in forest to a clearing, Vacherie des Erps (1749m.). Ignore a L-hand path to the Cerise lake and col. Take a small track in the same NNE direction in forest on L side of stream to a little pool above the forest (1945m.). The track goes up a grassy rib to a marshy shoulder, Sagnes des Erps ($1\frac{1}{4}$ h.). Above this a steeper section leads N to the lower part of the Guilié cwm, under the impressive rock spire of the Cayre des Erps, to R. At the head of the valley are two cols: on the R, Guilié, on the L, Mercantour. Follow a track in the grassy bed to a small black rock barrier ($1\frac{1}{4}$ h.). Keep R and go straight up again past a pool (2400m.), and aim directly for col over scree or snow ($1\frac{1}{4}$ h., $3\frac{3}{4}$ h. from Le Boréon).

On the Italian side descend slightly to a vantage point rather to the R (N). To the N, the W ridge of Brocan comes down to finish in a sharp rock tooth. Descend slightly and traverse N across the Vallone di Ghilié, snowbeds and a stream, then contour N without rising, to the foot of steep rocks of the aforesaid tooth. Go L along the base of the rocks to the far side and ascend scree to a shoulder of large blocks (2747m.). Continue N, descending slightly and cross the narrow valley (snow) coming down from the Colle del Brocan. Traverse smooth rock banks under the W side of Bastione, then more large blocks lead to the tiny Lago di Nasta (2800m.), directly below the S side of the Cima di Nasta ($1\frac{3}{4}$h.). This often snow/ice covered tarn is not properly marked on any current map. Descend to the L (W) beside waters flowing from the tarn, on L side of a long broad gully with smooth rocks. At the bottom of the main gully section, traverse out R round the base of the

Nasta to the hut promontory (45 min., 2½ h. from Col de Guilié, 6¼ h. from Le Boréon. A party with light loads and in good conditions could expect to make the excursion in 5½ h.).

20. From the Cougourde hut. Complicated route finding, somewhat steep, otherwise easy and shorter than R.19. Mostly trackless. I-/I.

From the hut follow the main track N, over the stream and under the rocky Gaisses slopes, up to the boulder plain of the Lac des Sagnes (2198m.). Leave the track and move L (W) across S end of the stagnant tarn. Up to the NW rises the Tête des Lacs Bessons (2688m.). Ascend straight up grass and rocks with small outcrops easily turned, as if aiming directly for this summit. On the R is a shoulder/ridge, similarly another on the L. Keep going uphill until continuous screes and rock bands encircle upper part of mtn. Move L (W) over grassy/stony ground and go round the L-hand spur, traversing and ascending all the time to enter a very stony boulder cwm. This has two small tarns in it, hidden in hollows (2516m.) which can be missed (but doesn't matter) among the long stony ribs. Head N in the line of these two tarns then trend L over or round rocky hummocks to reach in a big hollow below continuous rock slopes of the Tête de la Ruine, the fisherman's paradise of the Lacs Bessons (2545m.) (1½ h.).

Follow round the SE banks of the twin lakes, up and down over smooth rockbands, and cross the main outfall (2541m.). Move L (W) above the outfall and climb somewhat R on a steep grassy spur with a small track up rockbands. The angle eases after 10 min. Slant progressively L, leaving the line of the spur to your R, and commence an easy rising traverse L (NW) to enter a shallow rocky defile lying parallel with and still some distance above the Baissette sub-valley below. Opposite (NW) is the imposing peak of Cime de Baissette - a good general indicator for direction up to this point. Follow the defile, snowbeds then rocks and scree always in a slightly ascending traverse until the stream in the Baissette valley is close to hand. Traverse NNW to join it just before reaching the larger of the two Baissette tarns - invisible in its hollow almost until you get there. Straight ahead (N) is the imposing snowy cwm (2724m.) of the Guilié-Ruine summits; ignore. Cross a boulder shoulder just before and L of the first tarn, then rocky level ground due W to the smaller second tarn in a few min. This tarn marks an important, unsuspected saddle/col, the Baisse de Baissette (2650m.), giving access to the Guilié valley cwm (45 min.).

Move W beyond the second tarn and descend into the Guilié cwm bearing a little R over stony terraces and grass. Keep as high as possible without getting involved with rougher terrain up to the R. Go down for 200m. to c.2450m., then traverse to the cwm bed where R.19 is joined and followed to the Col de Guilié (1 h., 3¼ h. to col). Continue by R.19 to Remondino hut (2½ h., 5¾ h. from Cougourde hut).

Bozano 2453m.

CAI. Probably the most important hut site in the Italian zone, situated in the upper part of the Argentera valley below Corno Stella and adjoining W face of the Argentera itself. Hut modernised in 1967, and fully equipped, dormitory places for 40. Door normally locked, keys at the Albergo Turismo in Terme di Valdieri.

21. From Terme di Valdieri the rough road in the Valletta branch valley is followed to the Gias delle Mosche (1591m.), 4 km., 1 h. on foot. Carparking area. Signpost for hut just beyond chalet, path N10. The small track soon mounts steeply in forest to emerge at the Gias del Saut (1847m.). It continues steadily above L side of the Argentera stream gorge to the Gias del Mesa (2070m.), thereafter on slopes to N in zigzags to hut ($2\frac{1}{4}$ h. from Mosche chalet). I-.

Questa 2388m.

CAI. Situated on N shore of the Lago delle Portette, adjacent to the Cresta Savoia and Préfouns group. Fully equipped, 32 places, door locked, keys at the Albergo Turismo, Terme di Valdieri.

22. From Terme di Valdieri a rough road in the Valasco branch valley is driveable for 6 km. to the second large bend in the upper valley, just after the Ponte Valasco (1814m.), under grassy rock terraces that support the Lago delle Portette to S. Carparking, 2 h. on foot. Starting up a steep zigzag track, reach in 20 min. a fork R (1996m.). Now continue direct through an outfall depression in the slabby terraced slopes to a T junction at top, hunters' path N22. Go either side round a pool and cross grass to the hut above lake shore ($1\frac{3}{4}$ h. from road). I-. All maps at present are imprecise for this approach.

23. From Col de Salèse (R.12) over the Pas du Préfouns (2615m.) by R.112, $3\frac{1}{2}$ h. Has little interest; parties in France wishing to climb in the Préfouns group normally start from the Col de Salèse.

Jacques Guiglia bivouac (2437m.). CAI. Situated on a knoll between the middle and inner tarns strung along the large terrace on the immediate N (Italian) side of the Fremamorte col, as noted in R.108. Keys at Albergo Turismo, Terme di Valdieri.

Note:
Italian hut keys are also available from G.B.Piacenza in Sant'Anna di Valdieri.

Merveilles region

General

Mont Bego (2872m.) is the first lofty summit encountered on entering the central part of the region from its E side in France. This approach is made from the Roya valley which carries the main road from Nice to Italy over the Col de Tende.

24. St.Dalmas-de-Tende (696m.) in the Roya valley is 80 km. from Nice, frequent bus service; hotels, proper campsite, shops, etc. From here a small metalled road goes W up the Bieugne valley to les Mesches (1390m.) in 10 km. Mini-bus service, carpark, one inn. Two valleys continue into the mtns: Minière (W) and Castérine (N).

Minière valley

25. The L (S) side of this forested valley is traversed by a jeep road right up to the CAF Merveilles hut (2111m.) in 7 km. Otherwise $2\frac{1}{2}$ h. on foot from les Mesches. Jeep hire at les Mesches, a busy service in summer for day-trippers and others visiting the Merveilles engravings. The hut is built on S shore of Lac Long Sup., adjoining entrance to the Merveilles valley; warden, restaurant service, 85 dormitory places. A stage on GR52 and a variation stage of the classic high level route. Mt.Bego rises directly N.

Castérine valley

26. The small road out of les Mesches continues good for 3 km. to Castérine hamlet (1543m.), two small hotels, bunkhouse, mini-bus service. To the W rises the Fontanalbe valley which is entered and traversed both sides by a circular jeep road. Jeep service by reservation at hotels, passable for small cars, but latter discouraged. Mt.Bego rises above head of Fontanalbe valley, to WSW.

On the L side of the main valley the jeep road runs N over a shoulder (1719m.) to a bridge (1676m.) at the entrance to the Valmasque gorge and valley, where the latter runs W from the top of the Castérine valley. (The jeep road continues on the other, NE, side of the valley to cross the Baisse de Peyrefique and eventually reaches the Col de Tende by a high level corniche under the frontier; one of the most hair-raising jeep tours in the Maritime Alps).

Valmasque valley

27. Near the shoulder (1719m.) in the Castérine valley another jeep

road branches L and contours forest above the bridge crossing point of
the first road, and goes into the Valmasque valley. This small road,
rough stony surface but feasible for most cars, continues up the L (S)
side of the valley to cross its stream at pt.1969m., finally reaching the
Julie cabin (2027m.), carparking area. Now on foot by a tractor road
in zigzags S, then returning N along a rocky terrace past a junction
L (ignore) up to a dam wall across Lac Vert and the CAF Valmasque hut
(2221m.) on a hillock at its N end. Rebuilt in 1985, warden and restaurant service, 55 dormitory places, 1 h. or less from Julie cabin, as
several shortcuts are possible; 3 h. all the way on foot from Castérine
hamlet. A stage on the classic high level route. Mt.Bego lies to S.

Rock engravings

28. These are very extensive and varied. They are found in two main
areas and in several lesser ones; notably round the small lakes in the
Merveilles and Fontanalbe valleys, on the SW and NE sides respectively of Mt. Bego. The Diable lakes valley WSW of the Merveilles
hut contains another group of engravings. All the sites are less than 1 h.
walking distance from the Merveilles hut or jeep roadheads.

Nearly 50,000 images carved in rock slabs and walls have been identified and classified. This work by primitive peoples, thought to have
commenced c.3000 BC and continued up to the Roman occupation at
the time of Christ, represents scenes and symbols of their times and
reflects in artistic technique the progress of their civilisation through
the classical pre-history ages of stone, bronze and iron, down to the
Roman age. The race occupying this zone over such a long period is
generally named as the Ligurian tribe; similar inscriptions, though nowhere nearly as extensive, have been found in other parts of the SW Alps,
and suggest that related tribes were identically active. The engravings
show these people to be dominated by a religious code administered by
various chiefs and headmen. Agricultural activities were the mainstay
of the community. Old field enclosures were identified in this part of
the region before the progressive discovery of the rock engravings sites
at the end of the 18th century. All the sites are situated above 2000m.

and many early visitors in the 19th century failed to find them. An English botanist, Clarence Bicknell, was first to commence a systematic study of the work, between 1880 and 1918.

All the sites are protected under French law; anyone caught damaging or trying to deface the images is liable to imprisonment and heavy fines; wardens patrol the main sites. Prior to legislation in the 1930s, most attempts at theft, to cut away and transport the massive rockslabs, failed, although some of the work has been spoiled by graffiti. The latter inane habit of the modern tourist is the 'criminal act' that the wardens are anxious to deter. Where engravings appear on rock at an angle that can be walked upon, ice axes, walking sticks and the like, camera tripod feet and footwear shod in nails or leather must not be carried or used. Vibram soled boots are permitted, as are gym shoes or any rubber soled footwear.

Camping in the designated zones of the Merveilles and Fontanalbe is forbidden - the limits are marked out on the ground for the former. At points along footpaths large white asterisk pointers indicate the location/direction of some of the most important engravings, but these are not entirely comprehensive. Pamphlet guides for the engravings can be bought at the Merveilles and Valmasque huts, at Castérine, les Mesches and St.Dalmas-de-Tende.

The images consist of engraved drawings on coloured rock slabs, the oldest being quite faint and the most recent quite bright. They represent: horned heads of cattle (many sizes), plans of settlements - field enclosures with dwellings and figures deployed in workaday occupations, agricultural implements, objects of worship such as sacrificial animals, collections of axes and daggers; above all figures that dominate the community - priests, sorcerers, labourers at work. Phallic symbols and fertility are depicted in several ways.

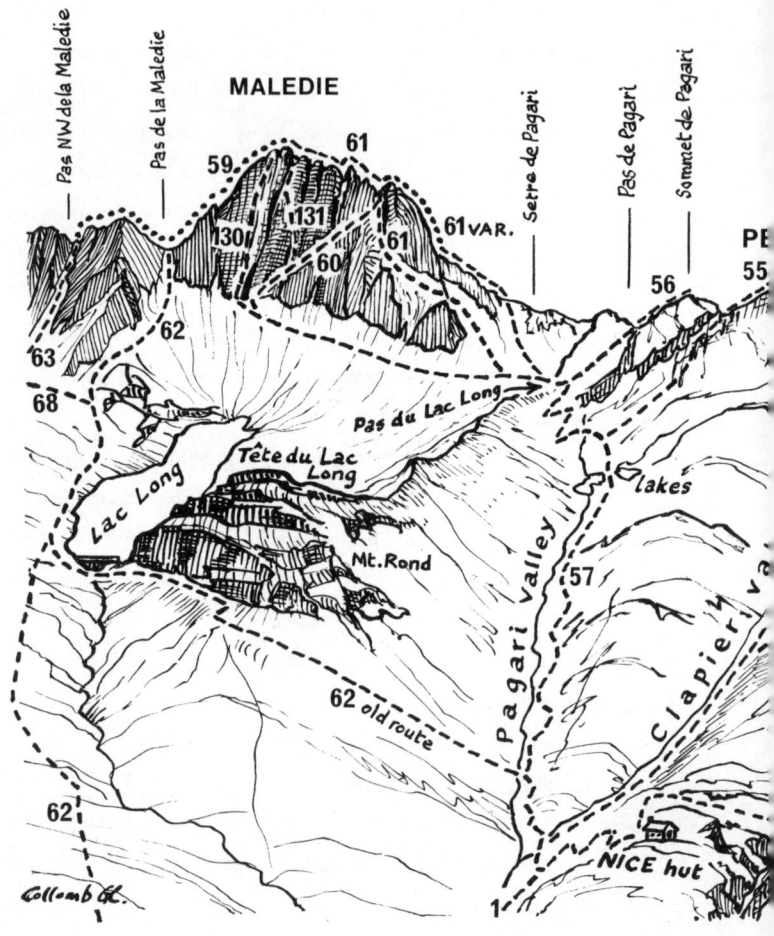

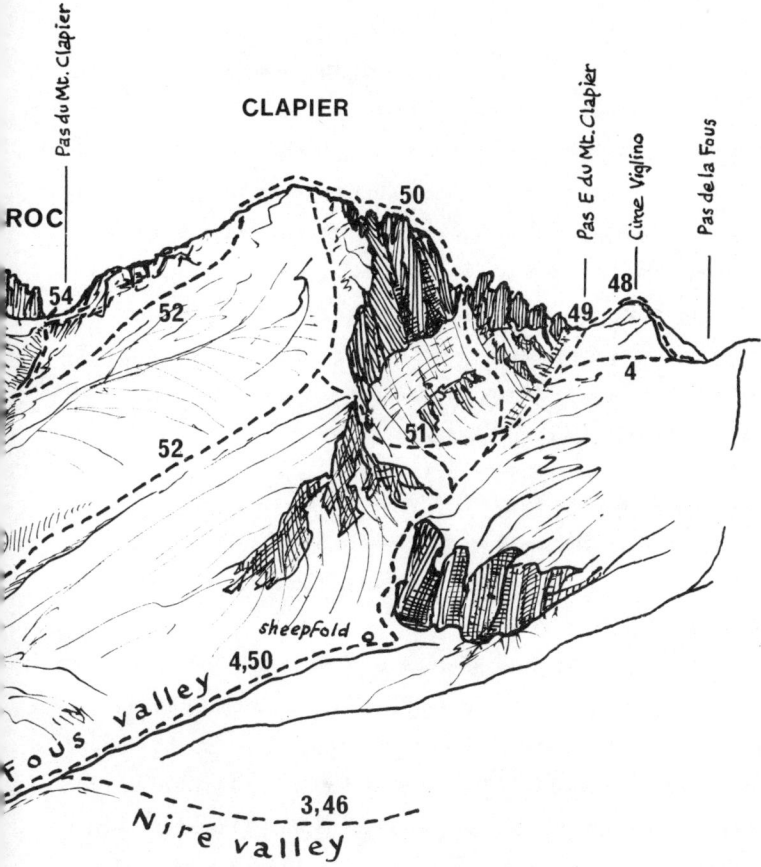

Locations

29. Merveilles zone: either side of the double path running up to the lake at 2294m. (R.3), among them the rock tablets known as the Christ, Chef de Tribu, the Autel and the Sorcier. The engravings are spread over considerable distances in very rough rocky terrain and a precise route guide is needed to locate particular sites without a time-wasting search. Fontanalbe zone: round the two small lakes at 2200m., and across the rough slopes of the Chiape de Fontanalbe. Diable zone: around the shores of or between the following lakes, some of which are now damned for hydro-electric purposes (the sites are protected and marked by 'star' indicators): Fourcat, Carbon, Moute, Trem, Mouton, Huile. In all zones steep rockbands and outcrops divide some of the site levels. One must traverse rather than go straight up or down between different levels - indeed the technique one must employ to make progress in so many parts of the region.

Access to Merveilles hut from St.Martin-Vésubie

30. Two possibilities occupying (exclusive of time spent on roads) much the same walking time, but disparate distances and vertical intervals ascended/descended.

The most interesting route, preferable for those with their own transport, involves a 10 km. stage of GR52, with total ascent intervals amounting to 600m. (more in reverse direction). From St.Martin by road down to Roquebillière, then up to la Bollène and the Col de Turini (1607m.), 4 small hotels, 28 km. Mini-bus service in summer. Above Turini a small side road climbs to the ruined military defences called L'Authion (2080m.) in a further 8 km. No taxi hire above Roquebillière. From here follow GR52 to the N, clearly indicated on the map. The section from Baisse Cavaline to the Pas du Diable has only a vague track in places. $3\frac{1}{2}$ h. from L'Authion to hut.

The hut can be reached from the Gordolasque valley (St. Grat hamlet) by a good path over the Pas de l'Arpette (2511m.) in about $3\frac{1}{2}$ h. Considerably shorter in distance but the uphill ascent is sustained for over 950m. Both ways, 1-.

Mont Bego 2872m.

31. Signifies divine place for the worship of gods. An outstanding viewpoint. From the Merveilles hut cross the dam wall NE and go up grass and stone slopes of the SSE spur to a fore summit. Continue by a short craggy ridge to main summit, 1 (2 h.). From the plateau area just N of the lower Merveilles lake (2294m.), R.3, by grass and very stony slopes trending R all the way to S fore summit, 1 ($1\frac{1}{4}$ h. from lake). From the Baisse de Valmasque, R.3, by the N ridge over Cime Pollini (2735m.), experienced walkers only, 1 ($1\frac{1}{2}$ h. from saddle).

Gordolasque – Roya divide

BAISSE DE VALMASQUE   2549m.

Sorcerers' pass. Broad saddle between Mt. Bego and Mt. du Gd. Capelet, linking the Merveilles valley (S) and Basto valley (N), from the Merveilles hut to Valmasque hut. A variation of GR52 and of the high level route. Much frequented, snow patches to mid-July. Ice axe. I-.

32. From the Merveilles hut follow R.3 over the saddle (1½ h.) to the fork where a track for the Baisse du Basto goes L. Keep straightahead, bearing somewhat R to reach the E shore of Lac du Basto. At the N end descend in zigzags past a pumping sta. and continue round two large hummocks to circle the E shore of Lac Noir. From the end of the dam wall a tractor road slants above the S side of Lac Vert and crosses a shoulder under pt. 2294m. Leave the road at a corner just before this pt. and bear L on a small track descending NE over slabby ground above Lac Vert and straight down to the S end of the Lac Vert dam wall, where the tractor road is joined again. Cross wall to hut on far side (1 h. from saddle, 2½ h. from Merveilles hut, same time in reverse direction).

CIME DU DIABLE   2685m.

Simple summit and exceptional viewpoint almost in a direct line between St. Grat and the Merveilles hut.

33. From East-North-East. Good track except for final ridge, I-. From the Merveilles hut follow waymarked path winding up the Diable valley past the lakes of Fourcat, Trem and Moute to a T junction between the two, possibly dried up, Diable tarns. Bear R (NW) and take steep zigzag track to the Pas du Trem (2480m.) (1 h.). Follow a broken track up the N (R) side of the E ridge; about halfway up cross the crest and follow up the L side to summit (1 h., 2 h. from hut).

PAS DE L'ARPETTE   2511m.

34. Little alp pass. Between the Cime des Verrairiers and Mt. de l'Arpette, a fairly well marked track on both sides from St. Grat in the

Gordolasque to the Merveilles hut. R.30, note, and partly R.35.

MONT DU GRAND CAPELET 2935m.

More simply known as Gd. Capelet = big head. The most important mtn. in this group and the highest summit in the central Maritime Alps belonging entirely to France if the minor Cabret subsidiary tops of the Gélas are excluded. It has a prominent N peak, Cime de Muffié (2901m.), at an obvious ridge junction seen but not named on the map. First ascent not known, but before 1885.

South-East Side. Normal route from Merveilles hut, I.

35. From the Merveilles hut follow main footpath W to a waymarked junction in 10 min. near the small tarn of Lac Mouton. Bear L along a good track going up steadily towards the Pas de l'Arpette. At the last zigzag running S to this pass leave the track and go N up a pleasant grassy hollow under Mt. des Merveilles, to stones and a double rockhead at the top, called Cayre des Conques (2692m.). Work up to the L-hand top. From here descend trending R down scree to the narrow Pas des Conques (2651m.). Above is the S ridge of the mtn. Now traverse more or less horizontally over rubble terraces below ridge for 15 min., until rock barriers above relent, then climb steeply L to a small ridge saddle N of pt.2771m. From here make a rising traverse R over large rocks and easy outcrops below ridge and join the E ridge about 50m. from summit ($2\frac{3}{4}$ h. from hut).

In descent it is quicker from the Pas des Conques to go straight down steep slopes E, round N side of tarn 2513m., and round N and E sides of tarn 2431m., to descend the rock barrier below from the SE corner of latter tarn. So reach the rocky plateau on N side of lake 2294m. in the Merveilles valley where R.3 is joined (summit to hut, $1\frac{3}{4}$ h.).

North-North-East Side (from Baisse de Valmasque). A good route, direct from the Valmasque hut, and the shortest and most direct way from the Nice hut (over Baisse du Basto). I.

36. Reach the Baisse de Valmasque from the Merveilles hut by R.3 ($1\frac{1}{2}$ h.), from Valmasque hut by reversing R.32,3 ($1\frac{1}{2}$ h.), from Nice hut by reversing R.3 (3 h.).

From the Valmasque saddle follow a track below rocks on the R side of the ridge rising to W, and after 20 min. cross a saddle in the ridge to descend round rocks on S side. Now ascend grassy rocks W in a steep hollow rising below the Muffié rocks. Near the top trend L and climb the NE facet of the mtn., over a series of terraced outcrops, trending L to reach the summit direct ($1\frac{1}{4}$ h., $2\frac{3}{4}$ h. from Merveilles and Valmasque huts, $4\frac{1}{4}$ h. from Nice hut).

From Gordolasque Valley (over Baisse du Lac Autier). The shortest way for parties based at St.Martin, with transport to roadhead. Ice axe before September. Quite frequented. I.

37. From carpark at Gordolasque roadhead (1800m.) follow the path of R.1 for 5 min. to where a track forks R (rock waymark) and winds up grassy slopes with rock outcrops to E, trending constantly R at first, then L to contour towards the Autier stream which is followed up on the R (S) side to Lac Autier (2275m.). Go round S shore of lake and above this ascend grassy strips on L side of valley, direction SE, to boulder slopes and old moraine. Slant a little R below moraine crest and enter the gully rising to the prominent saddle. The scree/snow bed leads to a fork; take the steep L branch with snow to the Baisse du Lac Autier (2637m.) ($2\frac{1}{2}$ h.). Towards the Gd. Capelet climb the main ridge on steep rocks for only 20m. then make a long, slightly descending traverse L (SSE) between two rock barriers to join the ridge saddle above the Baisse de Valmasque on R.36. Small track in parts. Continue by R.36 to summit (1 h., $3\frac{1}{2}$ h. from roadhead).

West-North-West Ridge of Muffié. The most interest general mountaineering route for parties starting from and returning to the Gordolasque roadhead. II. C.L.Brossé, V.de Cessole with B.Daniel, 9 September,1901.

38. As for R.37 to Lac Autier. From SE end of lake ascend due S up a stony valley to the Brèche Cabri (2585m.), situated in the relevant ridge to E of Cayre Cabri (2649m.) ($2\frac{1}{4}$ h.). Follow the crest over a number of steep grassy steps, turning obstacles on the R (S) side, up to the Cime de Muffié (2901m.) (1 h.). Now follow the N ridge proper of the main summit; keep to grassy rocks on L (E) side, down to a sharp

little gap. From here descend L round a buttress on E side then follow up below steep rocks towards the crest again, and continue upwards, remaining below actual crest, to reach summit (30 min., 3¾ h.).

39. <u>North Couloir</u>. Rises above the old frontal moraine adjoining gully exit to Baisse du Lac Autier (R.37); go up moraine to R, cross a permanent snowfield becoming a steep snow slope under the snow/ice gully cutting the N facet of Muffié. Climb gully direct to top. With crampons, etc., II/II+. It is not the gully further R, rising to a gap between pt.2866m. and Muffié.

BAISSE DU LAC AUTIER 2637m.

40. Saddle between Mt.du Gd. Capelet (Cime de Muffié) and Tête S du Basto, from the Gordolasque roadhead to Valmasque and Merveilles huts. See R.37, 36. On E side a scree gully then grass can be descended directly to the junction of the Valmasque and Baisse du Basto paths. I-.

TETES DU BASTO 2794m.

41. Bastion heads. Three rocky summits, S (2767m.), central (2737m.), N (2794m.). The easiest routes are II, rarely climbed. Main ridge traverse N-S direction, with abseils into gaps, II with a pitch of III; complicated. V.de Cessole, V.Paschetta with J.Plent, 27 July, 1923.

BAISSE DU BASTO 2693m.

42. Important frequented crossing point N of the Têtes du Basto. R.3.

CAYRE AUTIER 2676m.

43. The first summit on a branch ridge running W from near the Baisse du Basto towards the Nice hut. Marked but not named on map. No special interest. Easiest routes, I+/II.

TETE DU LAC AUTIER 2740m.

44. Imposing secondary mtn. on ridge to SE of Nice hut. By W ridge, reached at the E gap of the Pas du Niré (2555m.) by a scree gully directly above Lac Niré (R.46), I- (1½ h. from Nice hut). E ridge, II. NW ridge and facet give good short rock climbs, about IV.

CIME NIRE 2666m.

45. Black peak. The terminal rock spire after Tête du Lac Autier, overlooking Nice hut. Normally climbed with latter summit. From W gap of Pas du Niré (as R.44) ascend E ridge to top, I (1¼ h. from Nice hut). Several technical rock climbs.

CIME CHAMINEYE 2921m.

Better known as Mont Chaminèyes = the chimneys, visually descriptive of its pyramid form seen from the Nice hut. One of the most popular excursions from this hut. Seldom climbed from Valmasque hut. First ascent: F.Mader, A.Viglino with M.Sassi, 10 September,1895.

Traverse. The usual way is to climb the NW face and descend the S side. Pleasant grassy rocks, gneiss, generally sound. I, two or three exposed places.

46. From the Nice hut take a track E up to a grassy trough on L side of a big rock hummock, then make a descending traverse by a small track to the Fous stream in a grassy plain. Cross stream (usually a plank bridge) and slant sharp R (SW) up a track soon returning L above a bluff commanding S side of stream. Continue SE between grassy bluffs and rocks to Lac Niré (2351m.). Follow track up L (N) side of Niré valley, past a series of small lakes. From the last lake (c.2400) ascend a little valley to its N, keeping to L side, below W side of the mtn. Go up to the foot of a stony rib dividing the upper part of the valley. Ascend the rib to just below the Pas du Chaminèye and below N flank of the mtn. on your R (1¼ h.). This flank consists of a large scree slope and broken rocks. Climb the R-hand (NW) edge. Quite soon traverse R and cross rock steps to a couloir. Make a rising traverse across this couloir to a second couloir; climb this on the extreme R to the N summit. On the R descend a ridge for a few m. to a gap. From just below gap on its R (W) side continue to the main gap between the two summits. Now go straight up to the S summit (45 min., 2 h. from hut).

Descend S ridge to its first gap on the R (W), then go down a rock/ grass couloir on the L side to grassy slopes which are crossed to the Baisse Montolivo (2748m.) at the foot of the S ridge. From this saddle descend SW for a few min., then W, to reach the highest lake in the Niré valley, where the outward route is joined ($1\frac{1}{2}$ h. to hut).

PAS DE LA FOUS   2828m.

47.   Fous = source (of stream). Between Cime Viglino and Cime Lusière, an important ridge crossing between the Valmasque and Nice huts. Also for Cime Viglino, see R.4,48.

Clapier-Maledie frontier ridge

CIME VIGLINO 2910m.

48. Cima Alberto Viglino, marked but not named on IGN, secondary summit with twin tops, a notable and recommended viewpoint, situated on frontier ridge above the Pas de la Fous and Pas E du Mt. Clapier. Invariably ascended as a diversion from reaching or crossing these cols, or while climbing Mt.Clapier. From Pas E, by W ridge over a fore summit, I-/I, 20 min. From Fous col, by S flank, I-, 20 min. See comment in R.4. First recorded ascent: A.Viglino, 10 September, 1896.

PAS (COL) EST DU (MONT) CLAPIER 2862m.

49. Between Cime Viglino and M.Clapier, from the upper cwm of the Fous valley to the Clapier glacier. At the top of the Fous cwm (R.50), head directly for small saddle between 1st gendarme on SE ridge of Mt. Clapier and the ridge/slope of Viglino. The last 50m. are steep loose rock (2 h. from Nice hut). On the other side step straight down on to the icefield of the fairly large Clapier glacier which has an average angle of 18°. Small crevasses in ice easily avoided. Axe essential, crampons useful. Both sides, I-/I. The glacier laps round below the impressive E/NE face of Mt.Clapier. A popular excursion is to traverse the glacier below this face, keeping some distance from its rocks (stonefall), to return on the far side over the Pas (Ouest) du Clapier (R.54), below which on the French side tracks of the normal descent routes from Mt. Clapier are soon joined. I.

MONT CLAPIER 3045m.

Clapier = huge blocks and scree, typical of the region. A splendid mtn., a conspicuous hulk from many viewpoints, itself one of the finest viewpoints in the entire range of the Alps. The superb panorama extends round and across the Piedmont plain, embracing the curvature of the Western and Central Alps for about 200 miles. The Matterhorn and Monte Rosa are prominent. Corsica can be seen in the Mediterranean direction. The well formed Clapier glacier lies at the foot of the NE face. Rock, gneiss. Climbed by all and sundry from Nice hut. First ascent: Capt. Cossato, 1832. In winter: V.de Cessole with D.Martin, J.B.Plent, 11 December, 1897.

South-East Ridge. The best of the ridges, classic, curiously overgraded in foreign guides. From the Pas E du Mt.Clapier the lower part of the ridge forms 3 gendarmes and other obstacles before the crest mounts regularly. This initial section is seldom done (IV). The crest is normally reached at a small gap beyond the last tower. II, a few moves II+. Not serious, well protected. Rock fairly good, some loose and jutting blocks need care, and loose rubble. First ascent: A.Bruno, G.Kleudgen, 8 June, 1924.

50. From the Nice hut take a small track E over grass into a trough between a rocky hillock R and slopes of Mt.Clapier L. Continue through trough, descending a little to grass and rockbands on the N side of the Fous valley stream. Stay on the L (N) side and follow up small tracks in grass to a sheepfold under rock walls closing the valley. Ascend L (N) up grassy tiers to a scree/boulderfield and slant R across this to turn the L end of the rock barrier above. A small track runs up rocks in this. At the top reach the broad entrance to the upper Fous cwm. Ascend directly towards the lower turreted portion of the ridge seen at the top; trend a little R (as for Pas de la Fous) to use small scree and grassy strips; cairns at long intervals. Higher up keep L near the rocky slope under SE side of mtn. Near the top work L up scree into a short shallow gully (I+) leading to a gap in the ridge immediately L of its last tower which has an overhanging yellow nose on its R (E) side. The pt. reached is at the foot of the continuously steep looking part of the ridge (2 h.).

On the L side of the crest, initially some 15m. below it, follow a series of pleasant ledges, corners and ramps leading up at same angle as the crest for several rope lengths, shortly reaching the crest which is followed without incident (II-) to a near-level section with small teeth. These are mostly turned on L (II) always near crest, latterly on R, up to a steeper bit. Climb this direct over blocks and jutting rocks (one overhang, II+) to a prominent shoulder, Cima Asquasciati (placed by IGN well off ridge at pt.2911, and reckoned as 3009m.); continue to its far end. Descend R over loose rock in a groove then down a short smooth slab, making an awkward landing on loose stones at its base (II+). From the gap so reached, traverse the slabby R (N) side of a gendarme using good cracks and finish up a short pitch on its far side at another little gap (II with moves of II+). Climb a short broken wall above (I+), exiting L and returning R at the top to the easy summit slope from where the top is reached in a few min. walking ($1\frac{1}{4}$ h., $3\frac{1}{4}$ h. from hut).

South Couloir. Normal route from Valmasque hut, over the Pas de la Fous (R.4). Equally convenient from Nice hut by R.50 approach. I.

51. Cross the Pas de la Fous and traverse horizontally to a rock barrier forming R flank (looking down) of the Fous valley. Turn it by ascending scree low down and go up to a steep hollow under cliffs. Climb a fairly long couloir on the L (others R and much steeper and quite difficult) on scree and broken rock steps, exiting on to the stony summit slopes ($1\frac{1}{4}$ h. from Pas de la Fous).

West and North-West Flanks. The shortest ways from Nice hut. The variant is slightly better. I-. More difficult to find tracks in descent.

52. From Nice hut go up R side of the narrowing Clapier valley to the NE (track) for about 20 min., then climb out to the R into a shallow stony side valley leading to the summit ridge just to the R (SE) of the top ($2\frac{1}{4}$ h.). Alternatively stay in the Clapier valley until it becomes very narrow, with steep walls on either side. Not far short of the Pas du Mt. Clapier climb out R (E) over huge blocks and work up stony slopes (traces of paths) to reach the summit ridge just L (NW) of the top ($2\frac{1}{4}$ h.).

53. North-East and East Faces. There are several poor climbs ranging from III to V-, generally on unsound rock. The one taking the obvious diagonal break (as seen from the Pas E du Mt. Clapier) is worth noting. III. Ascended by V.de Cessole, L.Maubert with J.Plent, 13 July, 1898. It had been descended by Coolidge and the Almers in 1879.

From the Nice hut by R.49 on to the glacier under E face. Traverse to foot of the slanting couloir and climb it to a platform. A slabby gully on the R is taken to a fork where the R branch gives out onto the summit slopes ($3\frac{1}{2}$ h. from Nice hut).

PAS (OUEST) DU MONT CLAPIER 2834m.

54. Col on the frontier ridge NW of Mt. Clapier. I-. As for R.52 variation from the Nice hut, and continue up narrow valley to the col. The Italian side is a narrow earthy couloir leading down to moraine, from where the glacier is reached ($1\frac{3}{4}$ h. to col from either side).

CIME DE PEYREBROC (PEIRABROC) 2947m.

Pointed rocky peak on frontier ridge. Its well chosen name means shattered rock. Good view of the Clapier and Maledie. First ascent as below.

55. <u>West Ridge.</u> V.de Cessole with B.Daniel, A.Fantino, 9 December, 1898. II. From Nice hut by R.57 to the Lacs du Mt. Clapier($\frac{3}{4}$ h.). Climb the big stony couloir between Peirabroc and the Sommet de Pagari, then follow sharp crest to top ($\frac{3}{4}$ h., $1\frac{1}{2}$ h. from hut).

CRESTA MANZONE

The short spur jutting NNE from Peirabroc's shoulder. The gap is the Colletto di Peirabroc (c.2780m.), then Pta.Pia (2795m.), Pta.Zoe (2765m.), Pta. Fanny (2740m.), and Guglia Manzone (2718m.), this last an imposing rock tower. From the Pagari hut, traverse by starting up a fine little snow/ice route on the W side of the Guglia (I+), then along crest taking in all the tops to the colletto (II-). From here down the E side couloir (I+). The W side couloir is more direct but more difficult and unpleasant. 5 h. for round trip. A.Frisoni with A.Piana, 19 August,1909. The Guglia also has a number of short technical climbs.

SOMMET DE PAGARI 2905m.

56. This top, not named on IGN map, gives magnificent views of the Maledie and its northern glaciers. By the W side, I-. A path follows the crest, then stones to the top, 20 min. from Pas de Pagari.

PAS DE PAGARI 2798m.

The chief pass over the frontier between Mt. Clapier and the Maledie, from the Nice hut to the Pagari hut. I. The name is a contraction of Paganini Dalpozzo, who maintained the official route over the Col de Cerise in the 15th century. The Pagari pass was a smugglers' route.

57. From the Nice hut descend a little and cross the entrance to the Clapier valley. Now go up a small track N into the Pagari valley.

Walk up the R side and pass between the Lacs du Mt. Clapier (2502m., 45 min.). Climb a riser between the streams feeding the lakes and follow a zigzag path up a grass slope L. Ignore the path going on to the Pas du Lac Long and go R to the col ($1\frac{1}{4}$ h., 2 h. from hut).

58. From the Pagari hut work up L of the glacier. The route then goes to the R, above and W of the lowest point (40 min.). I-.

CIME DE LA MALEDIE 3059m.

Maledia. Fine peak on frontier ridge; it resembles a needle from some viewpoints. Badly depicted on map. It gives better climbing than Clapier and has an imposing face above Lac Long. The name is probably a corruption of maudit = cursed, wretched, a reference to the massacres at the Madone in the Middle Ages. First ascent: E. & L. Maubert with J.B. & J. Plent, 23 July, 1895.

North-West Face. The ordinary route. An ice axe should be carried.

59. From the Pas de la Maledie (R.62,63) cross under the face to near a little lake. At the extreme L end climb snow or rocks further L, then a couloir and a little buttress which lead to a stony couloir and the upper slope of the mtn. near the summit (30 min.). In descent take the summit slopes as far R as possible, and descend the couloir furthest R. From Nice hut, $3\frac{1}{2}$ h. From the Madone, $4\frac{3}{4}$ h. Both, I+.

South-West Face

There are several climbs on this impressive face which is easily reached from the Nice hut by R.61 or 62, or from the Madone by R.67,68 in reverse. The easiest is described here.

Diagonal Route. II+, recommended. V. de Cessole with J. Plent, 10 June, 1904.

60. Start directly below the summit, towards the L end of the face. An undercut gangway line slants up steeply R, starting with a smooth slab. Higher up cross a big gully and continue the diagonal line on lighter coloured rock than that above and below. So reach three good

pitches, one passing below an overhang (the Mauvais Pas), to exit from the gangway up a gully (R.61) to a gap in SE ridge which is followed to top as for R.61 (2 h. from foot of face).

<u>South-East Ridge</u>. The classic route, pleasant, II. L.Maubert with D.Martin, 9 July, 1897.

61. From the Nice hut follow R.57, and as mentioned therein break to the L up a poorly marked path to the Pas du Lac Long ($1\frac{3}{4}$ h.). On the other side contour below the Serre de Pagari and start the climb about 50m. below the ridge crest. Cross a couloir L, which rises towards the first tower on the ridge. Continue rising L into another, better defined couloir and climb it to a jammed block forming a window. Go through this and reach the first ridge gap ($1\frac{1}{4}$ h.). Follow the crest, with a knife edge pitch, or keep just below on L side, to the summit (1 h., 4 h. from hut). In descent, going back through the jammed block window is not recommended (falling stones). Reverse the variation given below by an easy abseil from good belay points.

Variation. The first ridge tower can be climbed direct from the crest of the Serre de Pagari. Start up the R edge, then follow the crest. In the upper section of 50m. there are two slabs separated by a ledge (III).

PAS DE LA MALEDIE 2927m.

The pass at the foot of the NW rocks of the Maledie gives access to a terrace of large blocks above the Maledie glacier, where there is a tiny lake. I-. Ice axe useful.

62. From the Nice hut it is easiest to descend to the Lac de la Fous and follow its W bank to the trail fork shortly before the dam (R.1). From here a well marked path rises N below Mt.Colomb, passes through a grassy plain, then follows gullies among polished rocks up to the W bank of Lac Long (1 h.). Go along the lake about 50m. above water level, across an awkward loose rock slope to a little snowy valley at

ST. ROBERT

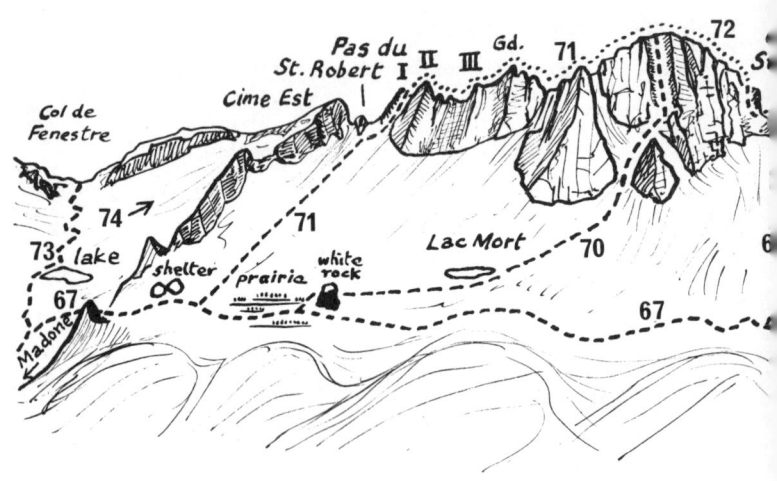

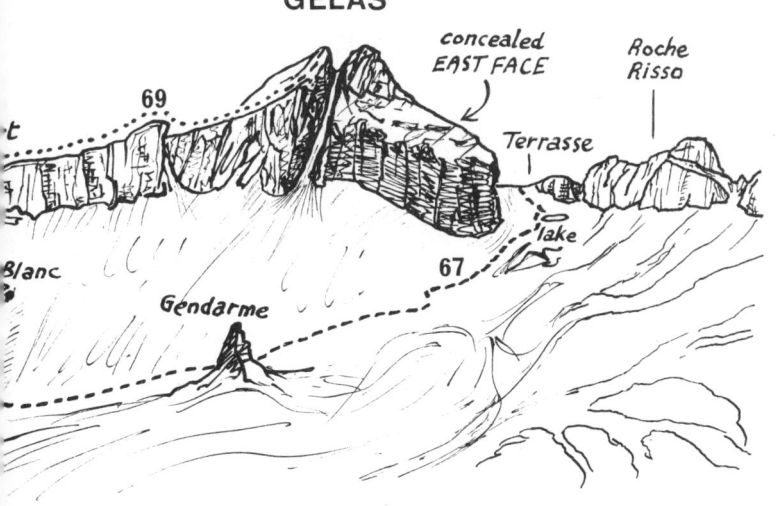
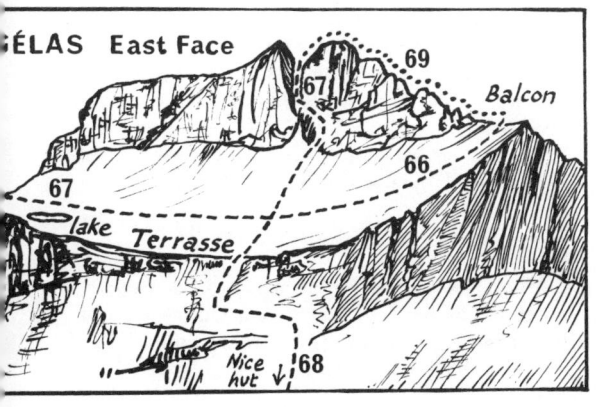

the N end, below the Balcon du Gélas. Contour R, round the foot of
a rock spur which divides the snowy valley from another, more open
cwm to the R. At the top a scree/snow couloir with blocks leads to the
Pas (3 h. from Nice hut). The old direct route to Lac Long by a rising
traverse, still well marked, under Mt. Rond, is not recommended, owing
to the delicate and awkward crossing of the lake outfall.

63. From the Madone follow R.67, as for the Gélas, to the Col de la
Terrace ($3\frac{1}{4}$ h.). Now descend a broad rock/grass gully to a scree terrace, which is followed N before some broken rocks can be descended
to steep snow above Lac Long. Traverse the snow beneath the rock barrier of the Balcon and reach a long scree/snow couloir coming down
from the Pas NW de la Maledie. Climb to the NW Pas and follow the
Italian side of the frontier ridge to the Pas de la Maledie (1 h., $4\frac{1}{4}$ h.
from the Madone).

COLLETTO DEL MURAION   2930m.

A low relief saddle between the Maledie and Caire Muraion, not marked on IGN. The S side is a 45° snow/ice gully flanked by smooth
slabby rocks where fixed abseil pegs have been fitted. It is reached
from the foot of the Maledie NE face, over the Pagari glacier, and is
climbed frequently by parties based at the Pagari hut. Axe and crampons essential, II+. The other side adjoins the Pas de la Maledie on
the frontier ridge. Traverse to it round a frozen tarn in 10 min.

CAIRE MURAION   2972m.

64. The name of this striking secondary summit means "rock peak
above the stone walls flanking paths". It rises from a spur running N
from near the Maledie, initially over the Colletto del Muraion. By
the short SW ridge from this col by a gully on L of crest, I, 20 min.
Therefore easily accessible from the Pas de la Maledie as a 30 min.
diversion from ordinary routes up/down the Maledie. Worthwhile for
fine glacier scenery and a superb view of the Maledie NE face.
There are several technical climbs on the Muraion SE face.

Frontier ridge: Gélas-St. Robert

CIME CHAFRION 3073m.

65. The SW ridge can be climbed in 30 min. from the Balcon (II); turn a tower on the S side then follow crest. D.J.Chafrion produced a regional map in the 19th century. L.Maubert with J. & J.B.Plent, 11 July 1893.

BALCON DU GELAS 3085m.

66. For walkers dismayed by steep gullies, the balcony gives views comparable with those from the parent mtn., and for less effort. From the Madone follow R.67 to the Terrasse. Its screes and snow lead to the Balcon ($3\frac{3}{4}$ h.). A.Müller with B.Plent, 31 July, 1879.

CIME DU GELAS 3143m.

Second highest mtn. in the Maritime Alps, a distinctive profile with two tops - N and S (3138m.). The climbing is not particularly interesting but the ascent is very popular and the summit panorama wide. Rock, gneiss. Gélas = glacier. First ascent: P. & G. de St.Robert, C.Meynardi with G.B.Abba, A.Audisio, 17 July, 1864. In winter: V. de Cessole, E.Helbing, P. de Pas, A. de La Tour with J. & J.B. Plent, A.Ciais, 11 February, 1896.

<u>East Couloir (Normal Route)</u>. A completely safe, fairly long and gradual approach which picks a way over rough ground. Good rte. finding gives comparatively easy walking; axe useful. I+ for summit gully.

67. From the Madone follow the Col de Fenestre trail for 50 min., as far as a zigzag below a prominent black rock standing on a grassy plain (2171m.). Leave the path and cross a little grassy valley to R(E) and rise slightly to a small but distinctive col (2200m., 20 min.). Go over col then contour grassy slopes (tracks); pass L of two rocks forming a shelter then cross a grassy plain (20 min.). The track now heads directly towards the mtn. Pass L of and above a large white pointed rock with black lichen on its top. The Lac de l'Isolette, with a little island, appears to the R. Pass to the R side of and a little below Lac

Mort (2527m.). Rise progressively over grassy rock bands with the Isolette always in view. Cross the Vallon Blanc (2550m., 40 min.) and climb a large hump on the far side by grass on the R. Cross a little col L of the Gendarme des Lacs Balaour (2707m., 20 min.). Continue rising slightly over grass and cross the Plaine de Rochers (10 min.). Now follow a spur of broken polished rocks to the E then traverse R along grassy ledges leading to the Lac de la Terrasse (2825m., 15 min.). Then snow and large rocks to the Col de la Terrasse (2945m., 20 min.). One has now passed round the foot of the S ridge of the mtn. and can look into the depths of the Gordolasque valley. Work towards the Balcon, seen at the head of the Terrasse, but soon move L to the couloir coming down the E side of the mtn. from gap between its twin summits. Climb snow or scree to rocks on its R and continue up them to a large terrace. Make a rising traverse L over rock steps to enter the couloir above its bottom pitch. Now climb rocks on the L side to the gap (35 min.). A step up on the R and a path lead to the top (5 min., 4 h. from Madone; 3 h. in descent). Remember that on the way down the rte. never heads directly towards the Madone, but always more to the R.

68. From the Nice hut take R.62 to the snowy valley at N end of Lac Long. Climb to the L above snowbeds over snow or scree and broken rocks to the terrace crossed by R.63. Cross this terrace to a large and grassy couloir which leads to the Col de la Terrasse ($2\frac{1}{2}$ h.), where R.67 is joined (45 min., $3\frac{1}{4}$ h. from Nice Hut).

Traverse of Main Frontier Ridges. The classic rte. along the WSW and NE ridges from the Collet St.Robert (2832m.) to the Balcon. Splendid views of big rock peaks and the glaciers on N side of the mtn. II. WSW ridge: L.Maubert with J.B.Plent, 1892. NE ridge: E. & L. Maubert with J.B.Plent, 1893.

69. From the Madone follow R.67 as far as the Vallon Blanc. Now work up past Lac Blanc (2665m.) towards the Collet St. Robert which is reached via an earthy gully ($2\frac{3}{4}$ h.). At first go along the L(N) side of the ridge, then follow the crest up a steep riser. Descend a crack to the L, just below an overhanging tower, then ledges and steps lead down to a stony saddle separating the lower part of the ridge from the upper mass of the mtn. Climb a couloir on the R, traverse R on little rock ledges then take slabs with good rock to the top (1 h., $3\frac{3}{4}$ h. from Madone). From summit go down the NE ridge, keeping R of a subsidiary top, to a step descended L of but near the crest. Cross the head of a large scree couloir, then a ledge system and rock gangways lead back to ridge below a yellow gendarme. Turn another gendarme on the L, then follow the broad easy crest to the Balcon (3085m.). Now scramble straight down to the Terrasse and follow R.67 back to the Madone, or R.68 to Nice hut. The NE ridge is alleged to be very loose now and R.67 from the summit may be preferred for the descent.

CIME ST. ROBERT   2919m.

Generally a more interesting mtn. than the Gélas. The rock is gneiss and usually sound. Named after Count Paul de St. Robert who first climbed the Gélas. First ascent: L.Maubert with J.Plent, 6 September, 1893. In winter: P.F.Rouyer with L.Orset, 13 March,1926.

South Side. The normal route, pleasant grassy rocks, I+.

70. From the Madone follow R.67 to the grassy plain ($1\frac{1}{2}$ h.) then work L to reach Lac Mort (2527m., sometimes dry). Directly below the summit and somewhat L a scree gully rises to an obvious hanging scree slope. Go up gully and R edge of the scree (conspicuous from Madone), then traverse R across the S ridge to enter a grassy gully further R, leading to the top ($1\frac{1}{2}$ h., 3 h.from hut). Or finish up the finer ridge (II).

West Ridge. A very popular, classic route with fine situations and continually interesting pitches, III+. V. de Cessole with A.Ghigo, 31 August,1911. Getting somewhat battered due to the large number of organised courses taken up it with guides in charge. Arguably the best climb of its type in the Mercantour Park.

71. From the Madone follow R.67 to the grassy plain ($1\frac{1}{2}$ h.), then turn up L for some distance towards the Pas du St.Robert at foot of the ridge. Before reaching this col take a slanting rock couloir rising to the gap between the 1st and 2nd gendarmes (30 min.). Climb the crest of the 2nd gendarme (III-), then descend a gully/ledge on R to the gap below, followed by the crest line over two steps (II+). Climb the 3rd gendarme by a crack on the crest, then by a slab above, to belay on a little shoulder (15m., III+). A rock staircase (II) leads to top of 3rd gendarme. Descend 2m. to the L and reach a gap (II+), then cross a sharp blade of rock by its crest, descend to a little gap and continue (III) to top of the Grand Gendarme. Descend one m. to the L and go down to another gap (one move of III). A short slab and a step lead to the top of the Gendarme en Eboulis. Traverse it and the steps which follow (90m., II with a section of III) to the foot of the Gendarme en Escaliers. The next section may be avoided by following a good ledge on L side of the ridge to a broad rock gully leading back to the crest (III+). However a crack on the crest, a descent along the edge of a rock blade then cracked slabs allow a gap to be reached by a 4m. traverse on its R side. Now follow the crest to an obvious platform (60m., III). Climb a short steep slab above (peg, moves of IV+, delicate) to another platform which is crossed to a crack R of the crest (III). From top of crack easy rock (II) leads to summit ($3\frac{1}{2}$ h., $5\frac{1}{2}$ h. from the Madone).

<u>North-East Ridge</u>. The complementary frontier ridge, invariably used in descent to traverse the mtn. II+. Descended by V. de Cessole with A.Ghigo, 10 July,1911.

72. From the summit follow the crest, then avoid the upper step by descending a rock couloir on the R. Rejoin the crest and cross it, then avoid a second ridge step by a scree couloir on the L(N) side. Continue down to the Collet St.Robert ($1\frac{1}{4}$ h.). Parties frequently continue to the Gélas by R.69.

COL DE FENESTRE   2474m.

A major ancient pass from St. Martin to Entracque, with military installations on the Ital. side. Originally crossed by a Roman road, then one built by the Benedictines. Only the two great wars of the 20th century have deterred aims to build a modern metalled road across it. From the pass Monte Rosa and the Matterhorn can be seen over the Piedmont plain. Much frequented by day visitors to the Madone.

73. From the Madone follow the zigzag trail above the chapel. It crosses the Vallon Rostagn (2070m.) and works up to a meadow which is the source of the Fenestre stream. The trail passes close to a pointed black rock (2171m.) then reaches the Lac de Fenestre (2266m.). Zigzags lead to the col ($1\frac{1}{2}$ h.). The Ital. side is fairly steep; snow possibly to late season. 2 h. to the Soria hut (see R.7).

CIME EST DE FENESTRE   2686m.

74. From a little beyond the Lac de Fenestre (R.73) a big side valley leads towards the peak. A rock barrier passed on the R (I) leads to beneath the rocky crest. A narrow grass band with grey rocks on its L edge mounts to the top (2 h. from the Madone).

CIME OUEST DE FENESTRE   2662m.

75. This can be reached from the Col de Fenestre (R.73) by turning the first rocks on the French side, then follow crest until it becomes steep with large boulders; turn these again on S side and climb a gully of big rocks to the top ($2\frac{1}{4}$ h. from the Madone).

Gordolasque-Fenestre divide

ROCHE RISSO   2954m.

CIME CABRET   2938m.

Highest pts. at the topmost (N) end of the divide where the ridge is detached from the frontier watershed at the Balcon du Gélas. Mainly simple scrambles to both summits, reached by obvious rtes. adjoining the normal approaches to the Gélas and Maledie.

MONT COLOMB   2816m.

A frequented easy summit and fine viewpoint. Colomb = long = far or distant mtn. First recorded ascent: V. de Cessole with J.& J.B.Plent, 28 November,1899.

South-West Flank. A pleasant walk amid striking rock scenery, I-.

76. From the Madone take R.2 to the Lac du Mt.Colomb (2390m., $1\frac{1}{4}$ h.), then work up a cwm NE to a scree gully leading up to a gap between the jagged W ridge of the mtn. and the steep flank of Cayre Colomb on R. The gully emerges on the main ridge S of the summit; ascend scree to top ($1\frac{1}{2}$ h., $2\frac{3}{4}$ h. from the Madone).

South Flank. Normal approach from the Nice hut, I-.

77. From the Nice hut follow R.2 in reverse as for the Pas du Mont Colomb, to within 15 min. of this col. Slant R (N) and ascend a long scree tongue leading to summit (2 h. from hut).

CAYRE COLOMB   2702m.

A tapered rock peak with a long horizontal summit and some good climbing. First ascent by an Italian officer about 1899.

Main Ridge Traverse. An entertaining little climb, rather grassy, but rock good. For climbers only. II+.

78. From the Madone or Nice huts reach the Pas du Mt. Colomb by R.2 (2 h. or $1\frac{1}{2}$ h.). The S ridge rises above. Contour base of first bit of ridge on the L (W) side, crossing grassy rocks, and reach the crest

CAYRE COLOMB   W side

Pas du Mont Colomb

at the top of the lower section, at a shoulder. Now climb an open grassy gully leading into a chimney which finishes at a narrow gap. A short chimney R (crux) leads to the sharp ridge which is followed with interest to the SE top (45 min.). Descend to a gap and climb two steps and a slab to another riser, which is avoided L. Finish up crest to NW top (30 min., $3\frac{1}{4}$ h. from Madone, $2\frac{3}{4}$ h. from Nice hut).

Descent: Go straight down the N flank over steep grassy rocks, a 10m. wall and steps to a gap. Turn a gendarme on the R (E) to reach Brèche Colomb (15 min.). From here descend steep narrow gullies on

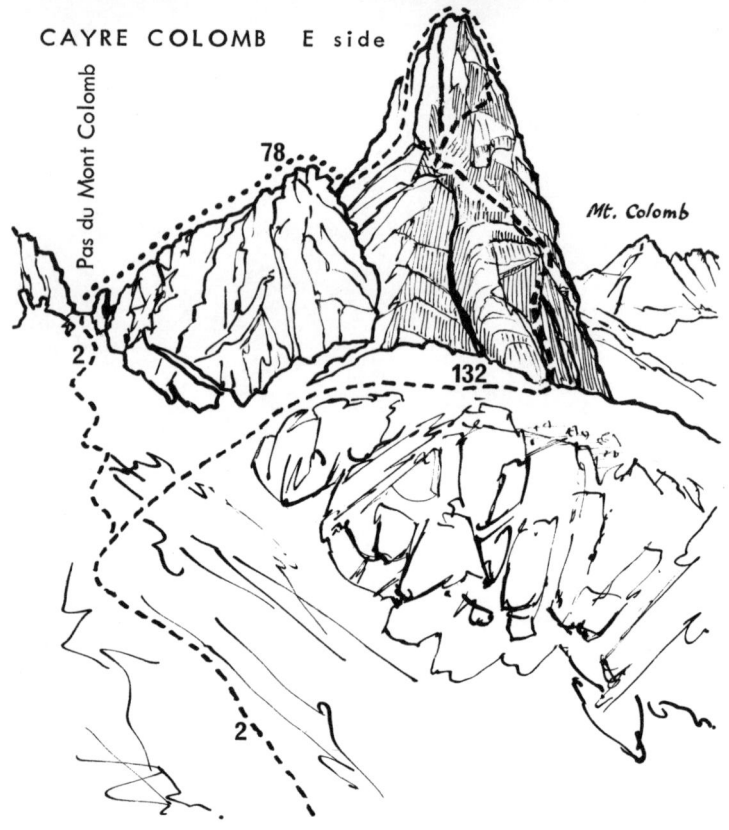

either side to regain the approach routes, I+.

PAS DU MONT COLOMB   2548m.   See R.2

MONT PONSET   2828m.

The large, attractive flat-topped mtn. dominating the Madone. Most splendid regional views and excellent climbing. The rock is gneiss and often lichen covered so that care is always needed in damp conditions. Named after a man who owned a pasture below the mtn. It was climbed by Jacques André about 1870.

<u>South Flank</u>. The easiest way, uninspiring, I-.

79. From the Madone take the path which passes church on its R, cross the Fenestre stream (bridge), then go up L side of the stream in the bed of the Ponset valley by a little track, to reach the marshy plain of the Sagnes du Ponset (2100m.). Continue up L side, turning little barriers, to the lower Ponset lake then the upper one (2415m). Now ascend L (N) over scree and grass to the summit ($2\frac{3}{4}$ h.). Descending in cloud, keep somewhat R on leaving the summit.

West Couloir. Also called the Z or diagonal rte., the classic way up. Seen from the Madone the W face is cut diagonally by a couloir rising from R to L. Its lower end finishes above the foot of the face; here also another couloir slants up from L to R. The V where the two couloirs meet is reached by starting R of the lower couloir and working back L. This scramble is more or less the quickest way up or down the mtn., I, with a bit of II-.

80. As for R.79 to the Sagnes du Ponset, then slant L over grassy terraces and finally climb a grassy promontory in the centre of the Ponset cwm to reach snow at foot of W face. Below the V junction of couloirs is another couloir reaching to the foot, with a chockstone and possibly snow. Start up the broad entrance to the couloir (snow), then cross R and make a rising traverse on its R side. Continue R over grass and rocks along the top of a stony section and a cone of rocks. Pass another little couloir with a chockstone, return R across it, go directly up its R side, then recross it above the chock. Continue L on grass, climb a little spur and reach the V junction. Start up the big gully on the L by climbing black rock steps L, then turn a big chockstone and roof on the L by slabs, or R up a buttress. Continue in the bed to top (3 h.).

CAYRE DE LA MADONE   2531m.

Colloquially, Grand Cayre. The prominent conical peak above the

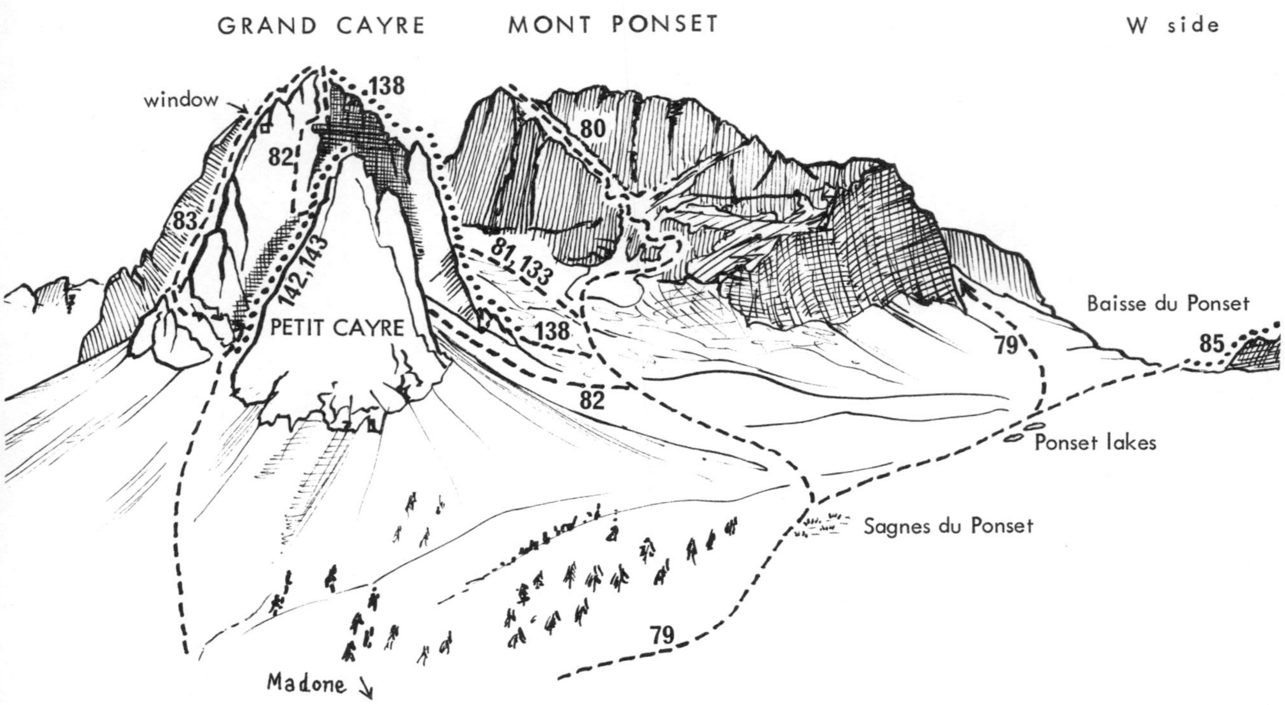

W side

GRAND CAYRE   MONT PONSET

Baisse du Ponset

Ponset lakes

Sagnes du Ponset

Madone →

window

PETIT CAYRE

80
81,133
138
82
79
85
138
142,143
82
83
79

Madone. According to legend an apparition of the Virgin Mary was seen in the window of the N ridge, following the massacre at the Madone in the Middle Ages. The window is clearly visible from the hut. Good rock climbs of all standards; the mtn. should be avoided during or soon after rain as the lichenous rock takes time to dry. Ascended at the end of 17th century by Ghibert.

East Ridge. The normal route, I+.

81. Take R.80 into the Ponset cwm on S side of peak. Cross the cwm to foot of the slope and couloir coming down from the Baisse du Cayre on R of peak. Avoid this couloir in preference for the next one L, falling from a higher gap in the E ridge, on the L of a big gendarme. The narrow grassy couloir leads to the Brèche du Cayre ($1\frac{3}{4}$ h.). Turn a little gendarme/step on the R (N) side, descending slightly, then climbing directly to cross the crest; move up L side for a short way before finishing by the crest (30 min., $2\frac{1}{4}$ h. from the Madone).

West-South-West Facet. The classic rte., short and picturesque, II. V. de Cessole with F.Martin-Titella, 27 August, 1915.

82. As for R.80 into the Ponset cwm on S side of peak. By a low line, cross to the foot of the wide, easy couloir coming down from the gap between the Cayre and Petit Cayre, and climb this to the Baisse du Petit Cayre ($1\frac{1}{4}$ h.). Descend a few m. on the other (N) side, then climb a secondary gully on the R to a terrace. Follow a ridge on the L which overlooks a steep ravine further L. A steep 10m. pitch on grassy rock leads R to a grassy hollow. Climb out on to the S ridge (R) and follow this to top (1 h., $2\frac{1}{4}$ h. from the Madone).

North-West Ridge. A good climb, passing directly over the window. 200m., III+, slippery when wet. G.Bonjean, F.Costantini, M.Laporte, J.Vernet, L.Wirz, 25 May, 1930.

83. Reach the foot of the ridge by R.2, 1 h.from the Madone. Start above the foot in the couloir of the Baisse du Petit Cayre; not far up

this traverse L to the crest by vague grassy terraces. Follow the crest
to a tree (25m., III). Climb 2m., traverse R for 2m. then cross slabs on
R side of crest to a platform with a tree (30m., III, delicate). Follow
crest to top of a gendarme (30m., II). Descend by crest to a gap and
continue up crest for 20m. to a platform (III). On the R climb a short
dièdre and a slab to a shoulder (15m., III). Now go along crest to top
of another gendarme immediately before the window (20m., III+). So
continue on steep crest above the window to summit (IV-, then III)
($1\frac{1}{2}$-2 h. from foot of ridge).

PETIT CAYRE   2413m.

84. The W buttress of the Cayre de la Madone, separated from it by
the Baisse du Petit Cayre. Popular practice ground for rock climbers,
1 h. or less from the Madone. The way up from the Baisse is obvious
and easy, similarly the couloirs below either side of this col (R.82).

BAISSE DU PONSET   2613m.

Between Mt. Ponset and Mt. Neiglier. See R.85. The E side is a
grassy couloir, I-.

MONT NEIGLIER   2786m.

A popular walkers' mtn. Neiglier = black. Rock, gneiss. Climbed
by Jacques André about 1870.

<u>Traverse by North Ridge and West Couloir</u>. A pleasant outing, I+.

85. From the Madone take R.79 to the upper Ponset lake (2415m.).
Continue up the valley to a grassy headslope ascended L to R to reach
the Baisse du Ponset ($2\frac{1}{4}$ h.). Go down a few m. in the couloir on the
other side, then follow a horizontal grassy ledge line under the N
ridge. Turn up a stony gully to reach a ridge gap. Move L across an
adjoining gap, linking the ridge to a buttress on the E side below, and
continue across a stony depression by a grass terrace to grassy rocks
which are climbed obliquely to join the ridge whose crest is taken to

N side

the summit (45 min., 3 h.). Leaving the summit, descend on N side of the W ridge for a few m., then cross it L and go down the large W gully on scree with two slabby steps (care required). At the bottom go down the Prals cwm to its tarns (2269m.). Instead of continuing down the valley to the Madone, it is more interesting to cross the Baisse des Cinq Lacs (2335m.) to the NW, a straightforward slope, descend to the Sagnes du Ponset and rejoin the approach rte. (2 h. from summit to the Madone).

<u>West Ridge Traverse over Pointe André</u>. A splendid, varied outing on mostly good rock, one of the best rtes. of its class in the Mercantour Park. III+. C.Jacquin, P.Piguet, 1938. Pte. André (2679m.) was first climbed by V.de Cessole with J.Plent, 27 May, 1904.
86. As for R.79 to the Sagnes du Ponset, where a clear track slants R up to the Baisse des Cinq Lacs ($1\frac{1}{2}$ h.). From this saddle work to the R (E) for some distance along the foot of the first big pyramid riser of the ridge (2611m.), small track, and just past it go up a grassy gully with some scree to the gap preceding the 1st steep gendarme. Climb it by a dièdre/couloir on the crest (III+). Descend to the next gap and go up to top of 2nd gendarme (III). Follow the ridge, cross a gap and descend a chimney on the R (III-). Traverse an easy step and climb the 3rd gendarme by a crack just L of crest (III+). Descend R to a shoulder, then move L to the next gap (II+). Climb a steep slab on the ridge (12m.), then a chimney on the L to top of 4th gendarme (III). Move to the R down to the next gap, continue along the ridge and climb a series of steps (II) to the top of Pte. André ($1\frac{1}{2}$ h.).

From the summit descend steep friable rock then turn several teeth with care by dropping down on the N side, followed by easier ground to Brèche André. (Escape down the couloirs on either side is II/II+, loose). From the gap either climb ridge crest as directly as possible (III+) to a peg and stance in 25m. Or work a few m. L along a grassy break to climb a short vertical wall to crest (III), followed by a steep smooth slab (5m., III+, crux). Above the peg stance steep, loose and sharp rock steps soon finish on the long, almost level ridge leading to Mt. Neiglier (1 h., $2\frac{1}{2}$ h. from Baisse, 4 h. from the Madone).

MONT CAVAL   2379m.
BAISSE DES CINQ LACS   2335m.

87. Caval is a corruption of "horse". A pleasant walking circuit from the Madone consists of going up to the Baisse by R.79,86 from where the Caval top is reached easily over its hummocky SE ridge. Return to the Baisse and descend S to the Prals tarns, then follow the outflow in to the Prals valley where a good path is followed back to the Madone. About 4 h. including Caval summit.

CIME DE PARANOVE   2556m.
PAS DU NEIGLIER   2442m.

88. The col is easily reached from the Baisse des Cinq Lacs across the Prals tarns cwm. From the col a grassy gully can be climbed to top of the Paranove.

CIME DE LA VALLETTE DE PRALS   2496m.
COL DE PRALS   2335m.

89. An important communication between the Madone and St. Grat. The mule path up the Prals valley takes $1\frac{3}{4}$ h. The adjoining summit can be ascended by branching R from the path, to a higher saddle (2339m.), then to the top by the grassy E slope. A steep path with many zigzags leads down to St. Grat in the Gordolasque valley.

BAISSE DE FERISSON   2254m.

90. A convenient link between the Madone and Belvédère, giving magnificent views of the Fenestre basin. Take the mule path towards the Prals valley for 20 min., then break R into the forest and the Moussillon valley. Continue up a wooded ridge and so to the saddle ($1\frac{1}{2}$ h. from the Madone). On the other side a path leads down to the Collet Carquière, thence a road continues to Belvédère. The ridge over Mt. Lapasse (2351m.), Cime de Clapeirette (2333m.), Cime de Font Frèye

(2334m.), or paths on their S flanks, Tête de Marre (2242m.) and Cime de la Palu (2132m.) with continuation to St. Martin, is well marked and provides a splendid 5 h. walk. In reverse this gives an interesting ridge walk of some length from St. Martin to the Madone.

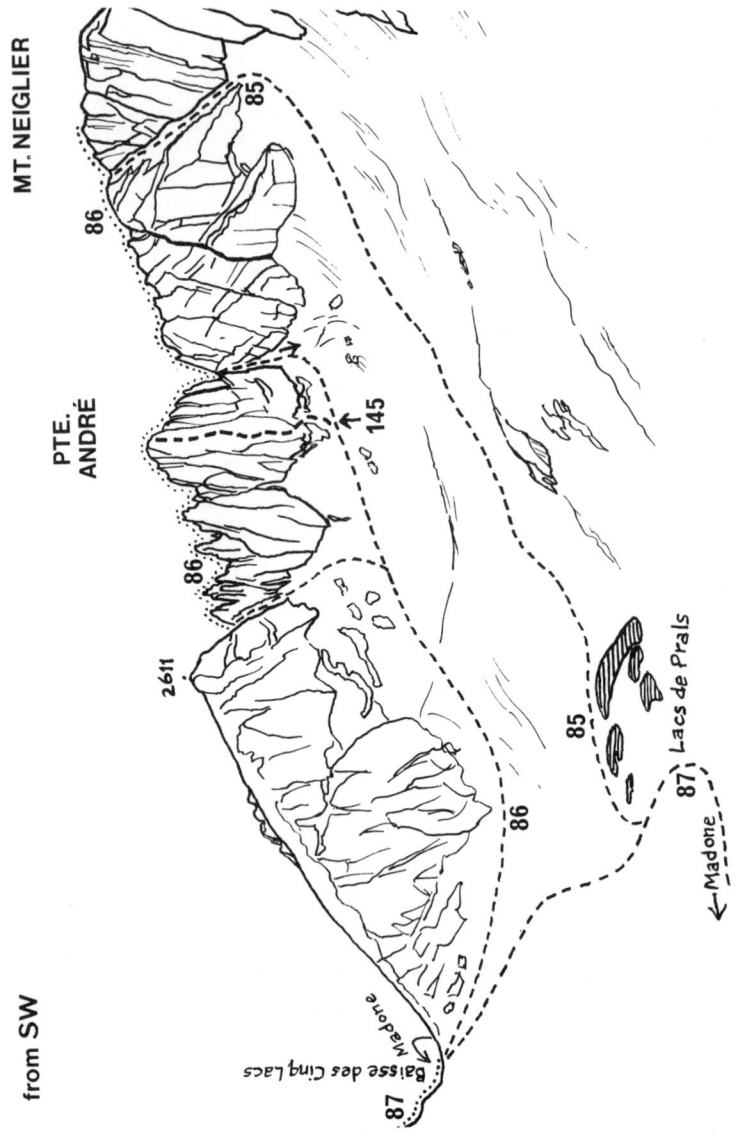

Boréon-Salèse basin

PAS DES LADRES   2448m.   See R.9

CIME DU LOMBARD   2842m.

Not often visited, easily attained as a diversion from the W side of the Pas des Ladres. Lombard is the NE wind coming from Italy into the Boréon basin.

94. <u>South-East Ridge</u>. An easy scramble, I-. From the Cougourde hut as for R.9 to the foot of the headslope and zigzags below the Pas des Ladres. A track forks L(N), cairn. Follow this into the Combe de Trecolpas and higher up, under the Bochetta Forno, turn a large bluff preferably on its L(W) side. Follow up the broad stony cwm bed to a short easy gully rising R to a gap (called erroneously on map, Baisse du Lombard) immediately after a prominent ridge tower (pt.2667m. is the next ridge peaklet S of this tower). Now either follow the crest or rubbly terraces and grass on R(E) side to top ($2\frac{1}{2}$ h. from hut).
A descent can be made into the Combe des Gaisses, fairly steep and loose, by going down the N ridge to the Brèche du Lombard, using short gullies, exposed terrace traverses and steps (I) on the E side. From the Brèche descend a short steep gully with two chockstones (I), to reach the cwm and follow down the bed to join at the bottom the initial outward part of R.9 near the hut ($1\frac{1}{2}$ h. in descent).

CIME DES GAISSES   2896m.

An attractive viewpoint, usefully combined with an ascent of the main Cougourde Peak 1.

95. <u>North Ridge</u>. Adds $1/1\frac{1}{4}$ h. from leaving to rejoining the route to the Cougourde. I. As for R.96 to below the last big blocks leading to the N gap. Leave the track and slant R across similar terrain to the S gap of the Baisse de Cougourde (2792m.), below a ridge step. Ascend grassy ramps, ledges and short steps L of crest to a slight shoulder, then follow crest on nice rock with short movements R to top (30 min., $2\frac{1}{2}$ h. from Cougourde hut). Note: The quickest descent is by the S facet gully, the top of which is reached from the summit in a few min. by steering slightly W of due S to the first opening on the L in the barrier above the Combe des Gaisses. Go down this (I) into the cwm and descend directly to hut ($1\frac{1}{4}$ h.).

Above: Cougourde from W.   Below: Pamela Collomb and Tony
Moulam on Cougourde Peak 4 after an ascent of the SW ridge (R.151)

CAYRES DE COUGOURDE 2921m.

A spur of 4 peaks projecting from the frontier ridge near the head of the Boréon valley, easily the most varied and one of the most extensive rock climbing sites in the Mercantour Park with routes of all standards. While easy of access in summer the steep slopes round its base, cut by rockbands, are avalanche prone in spring. The highest pt. is Peak 1 (2921m.) on the frontier ridge; the others are numbered running SW to Peak 4 (2892m.) which presents an impressive W face to the valley from where its profile resembles a gourd or pumpkin. Seen from popular vantage pts. this mtn. curiously makes little impact and its outstanding rock features can only be appreciated from close quarters. Rock, gneiss.

First ascent, Peaks 1,2,3: Count de Zassetzky with J.B.Plent, August 1890. Peak 4: J.Plent, 27 August,1895. Peak 1 in winter: V.de Cessole, P.Costa, J.Rouvier with L.Ciais, 27 December,1918.

Peak 1, South-East Ridge. By the Baisse de Cougourde (S. 2792m.); this rte. gives good views of the Entracque valley and the Gélas. I. An interesting extension is to follow the spur to Peak 4, II.

96. From the Cougourde hut the path crosses the stream and trends R to the Lac des Sagnes (2198m.). Ascend R with a small zigzag track and R of waterfalls coming from the Combe de Cougourde. Cross the combe stream high up to reach a balcony of steep rock at the foot of the broad SW ridge of Peak 4 ($1\frac{1}{2}$ h.). From here a grassy path hugs the base of the SE wall then scree leads to the L(N) gap of the Baisse de Cougourde. Keep slightly R of the crest on easy grassy rocks to top (1 h., $2\frac{1}{2}$ h. from hut). To continue to Peak 4, go along the crest and take a nice pitch astride a rock flake (II). Turn the gendarme in gap 1-2 on the R(N) and continue on S side to Peak 2. Work a few m. R then descend smooth boiler plates (II) above the R branch of the N face Y couloir, and continue on this side into gap 2-3. Now easy rocks on the S side to Peak 3. Take the S side again to gap 3-4. Turn the gendarme in this gap on S side and ascend just L of crest to Peak 4 ($1\frac{1}{2}$ h.). To return, use gangways of cracked slabs (II) on the N side to gap 2-3, then as the outward leg (1 h.). An alternative way to Peak 1 is the stony S couloir to gap 1-2 which has two jammed blocks, turned on R (II).

Peak 4, West Face (Z Route). The original frontal climb, crossing the prominent slab/terrace system cutting the middle of the face, classic and of considerable quality and interest. 400m., III+. G.&J.Vernet, 27 October,1927.

97. Approach as for R.96 to the marshy Sagnes tarn; ignore the usual track R and follow R edge of the plain near large blocks, rising towards a black barrier ahead, closing the valley above pt.2261m. Before this turn R up a steep grassy slope and at the top exit over a rockband (30m. I) to grassy ribs above. Follow up these trending R over several little rock steps to reach the foot of the W face of Peak 4 at the obvious gully coming down from gap 3-4 ($1\frac{1}{4}$ h.). Steep frozen snowbeds here to mid-summer. Start L of the gully and work up steeply from R to L by ledged cracks and short walls for about 100m. to where this system peters out. In a line of whiter coloured rock take a chimney (III+) on L, followed by slabs with good holds to a shoulder directly above; this is Cairn Jeannel, on the NW ridge of Peak 3. Now slant up R by an obvious chimney (15m., III+) to a small grass ledge. Join the central slab system on R, follow it, rising slightly, and cross gully 3-4 to a small terrace. Slabs mount R at $45°$ (III+) to a grassy balcony. Go down to a grass platform and follow this R to near its end. Now go up obliquely R over broken rocks to a vague gully on the SW ridge of Pk. 4, reached at an obvious gap. Take the ridge to top ($3\frac{1}{2}$ h. from foot of face). The shortest descent is by R.146.

CIME DE L'AGNEL   2927m.

A split rock cone at the head of the Boréon valley, a minor twin compared with the girdle of cliffs and shapely prong of the Cayre further W. Splendid regional panorama, popular with walkers.

South and South-East Flanks. The approach is from the SW. Confusing ground in poor visability, otherwise easy slabby rocks and scree, I-.

98. From the Cougourde hut the path crosses the stream and trends R to the Lac des Sagnes (2198m.). Contour the R side of this marshy area near large blocks and at the back go along bed on L side to where the Vallette Escure stream enters from the NW. A pleasant little track winds up the R side of this stream, some distance from it, then moves L into a horizontal gorge section to exit higher up beside a rock pool (2431m.) at a division in this secondary valley. Go up the R branch with a discontinuous track to the Lac de l'Agnel (2645m.) (1¾ h.). Now ascend grassy trods and rocks due E to reach the broad SW spur of the mtn. Take this for a short way, or on its R side, to a long, slightly rising and narrow grassy ledge line cutting right across the S flank. Follow this R between large areas of slabby rock at a glacis angle and at the end go round a blunt spur to scree and large rocks in a shallow hollow under the frontier ridge to R (E) of summit. Ascend this hollow rather tediously to a skyline shoulder then move L to top (1 h., 2¾ h.).

A worthwhile continuation is to follow down the rocky crest of the frontier ridge E to a saddle and onward along or near the crest with a few bits of I to the N top of the Cime de la Malaribe (2861m.) (1 h.). Return to the saddle then descend a rough but easy gully to rejoin the ascent route in the hollow of large rocks.

CAYRE DE L'AGNEL 2937m.

Due N of the Cougourde hut, the most conspicuous summit at the head of the Boréon valley, looking deceptively simple; in fact it has a complicated ridge and buttress structure. Agnel = sheep pasture. Rock, gneiss, generally poor for rock climbing though numerous technical routes have been made, especially on the Gd. Gendarme (2789m.) which adjoins the base of the S ridge and W face. First ascent: V.de Cessole, A.Vérani with L.Ciais, J.Plent, 26 July, 1910.

South-East Flank. Normally combined with the Cime de l'Agnel by peak baggers. Steep rocks and loose ground, I+.

99. As for R.98 to the Lac de l'Agnel. Ascend a steep scree slope diagonally R into a gully rising to a hanging screefield halfway up. Do

not enter the long straight gully L which lies in the summit line. Climb
this rock and grass gully to the screefield, then keep to L side for another 30m. under a little buttress, until you are level with the top of it.
Now move L and climb a rock ramp rising rather more steeply, parallel
with and above the gully screefield. Continue this line up a subsidiary
gully to exit on steep earthy ground under rocks of the E ridge. Make
a rising traverse L with a small track in parts and finish horizontally at
a little gap in a prominent subsidiary ridge coming from the E ridge not
far above. On the other side descend a gully for 20m. into a rocky
bowl under SE side of the summit. Ascend this keeping slightly R to the
E ridge in about 50m., then move L to top ($2\frac{3}{4}$ h. from hut).

South-West/South Ridge. The classic route, an excellent scramble
amid fine rock scenery. II+. First ascensionists.

100. Approach as for the usual way; shortly before the Agnel lake
make a rising traverse L over steep scree to the cone at the foot of a
steep gully coming down from the gap dividing the Gd. Gendarme from
the ridge. This is the last and shortest gully on the L along the SE base
of the mtn. Go up grass and rocks in bed to gap. The ridge crest line
lies to R. Climb a wall R in short steps (II+/III) to join the crest above
an initial step. Turn the next step by a terrace/ledge system L into a
gully and climb this (II+) to exit at a small ridge gap. Now follow the
slabby crest with flakes and pinnacles (I+) to a forepeak. Descend R
to a little saddle and finish up the summit ridge keeping R ($3\frac{1}{2}$-4 h.).

COL DE LA RUINE 2724m.

Ital. Colle della Rovina. An important pass over the frontier from Le
Boréon to Entraque. Crossed by the military in the 18th century and
probably known long before. Both sides, I-.

101. Fr. side, as for R.98 to the rock pool (2431m.); continue NNW
up the very stony U-shaped Vallette Escure, under W face of the Cayre
de l'Agnel, to a steepening where zigzags lead to saddle ($2\frac{1}{2}$ h.).

102. Ital. side. A good path leads from the Genova hut along terraces above the Lago Brocan to a rib with several rock bluffs which is followed easily in many zigzags to col at the top. Frozen snowbanks to mid-season make an ice axe essential (2¼ h. from Genova hut).

TETE DE LA RUINE 2984m.

Literally crumbling rock and earth. A mtn. walking objective with superb regional views, quite rocky and complicated ground, and contrary to French claims ascended more frequently than the Cime Guilié which is attributed with an even better panorama. Visits to Guilié probably outnumbered those to the Ruine before the Cougourde hut was built (see below). The ridge between the Ruine and Guilié is recommended by the French as a quick link for excursionists, but the short steep descents into gaps and exposed movements round tottering towers in the first part will be too unnerving for most walkers. II.

South-East Flank. The usual route. Finding the way in poor visibility could present acute problems. A rough scramble, I.

103. From the Cougourde hut approach by R.20. After two small tarns (2516m.) keep R in the stony bed and so avoid working L to the hidden Bessons lakes. Ascend scree trending R to the saddle of the Collet des Lacs Bessons (2647m.). Now traverse L and slightly downwards below a rockband, then return R up scree and blocks for a short way to the edge of a broad sloping terrace area with pt. 2843m. directly above, stretching L below steeper ground under E ridge of the mtn. Traverse L easily across this rocky area, rising a little with several slabby patches, to where the first rockband above is breached at a narrow spot somewhat before the summit line. Go up this R to a light-grey hanging scree field which is ascended trending L to a vague gully depression of reddish rock rising L to the S ridge not far from the top. Take steep shattered rocks in or near the shallow gully and halfway up (40m.) make a rising traverse R over similar ground to exit on the summit ridge a few m. from the top (3¼ h. from hut).

<u>South Ridge</u>. Slightly longer, useful for varying the return leg to hut.

104. As for R.20 all the way to the first and larger of the two Baissette tarns. Turn sharp R (E) and go up slabby ground pleasantly to large hump marking end of S ridge. Follow broad ridge on similar terrain to where rock steps occur. Traverse horizontally R below these on E side, keeping close to their base, latterly up a grassy ramp which leads into a gully depression similar to the one taken by R.103, and joining the latter exactly where you leave it for a rising traverse R to reach the top. A few moves in this short gully are I+ ($3\frac{1}{2}$ h.from hut). To attain Cime Guilié in the same day, reverse S ridge to the Baissette tarn and follow last part of the next route ($1\frac{3}{4}$ h. from summit to summit).

CIME GUILIE 2999m.

The highest summit on the horseshoe frontier ridge round the Boréon valley, hidden behind the Ruine (q.v.above). Traditionally the most visited peak in the area. Magnificent panorama. The name equates to "stream", that draining to the NW.

<u>South Flank</u>. The usual route, I-. Ice axe advisable. Note: From the Peirastrèche chalet (1936m.) on R.11 to the Cougourde hut, a well engineered path mounts along the R side of the Vallon Sangué and exits R up steep rocks from the continuation Vallon des Lacs Bessons to finish at the latter's outfall where R.20 can be joined. In fact by this approach it would be simpler to finish up the Vallon de Baissette branch, mostly trackless. Equally adoptable for the Tête de la Ruine.

105. From the Cougourde hut as for R.20 all the way to the first and larger of the two Baissette tarns. Bear N into the stark boulder cwm with old snowbeds below pt.2956m. Follow the bed then rise L above rock pool 2724m. and reach the S edge of the summit plateau zone. Ascend this directly to a short final slope and the top ($3\frac{1}{4}$ h. from hut).

BAISSE DE BAISSETTE   2650m.   See R.20

CIME DE BAISSETTE 2822m.

Prominent landmark in the area approached by R.20, composed of unpleasantly steep and tedious slopes of rock and grass.

CAYRES NEGRE DU PELAGO N.2745m. S.2741m.
MONT PELAGO 2768m.
CAYRE DES ERPS 2501m.

Pelago = dry. A ridge of peaklets forming a large secondary chain and spur coming down from the frontier ridge into the Boréon valley. Some interesting exploratory scrambles and rock climbs, in general not suitable for mtn. walking parties. A lot of grass and short pitches in access gullies. The W flank below Combe Guilié (R.19) is dominated by the conspicuous plinth of the Cayre des Erps which has numerous technical climbs of considerable character and interest.

COL GUILIE 2639m.   See R.19

COL DU MERCANTOUR 2611m.

Separated from Col Guilié by the Rocher de Guilié (2690m.). As for R.19 to below latter's final slopes, then bear L steeply to col.

CIME DU MERCANTOUR 2772m.

Mercantour = bad contour. The chosen centre of the French national park area, in reality a secondary summit thought long ago to be the highest peak in the Maritime Alps because it was mistaken for the apex of Argentera when viewed from the Vésubie valley. Nowadays a recommended excursion from Le Boréon; the cwm below the Cerise col is the habitat of a new breed of chamois imported to the park recently.

106. From Le Boréon follow R.19 to the first small crossroads of paths (1588m.). Take the L fork which traverses towards the Vallon du Cavalet then mounts through forest on its R side quite steeply with a switchback to join another path continuing N to cross the valley stream higher up. Numerous zigzags on the L side eventually merge at an old moraine running up to the Lac de Cerise (2223m.). Continue over the riser behind this tarn to the foot of the next zigzags a few min. away ($2\frac{1}{4}$ h.). Leave the path and ascend scree R (NE) to enter a cwm that

contains the Lac du Mercantour (2454m.). Go round S side of lake and above the NE shore ascend grass and scree slopes directly towards the summit. Follow up a brow to the top (2 h., 4¼ h. from Le Boréon).

COL DE CERISE   2543m.

An important pedestrian pass from France to Italy; the path was originally constructed by Buschetti in 1430. From Le Boréon as for R.106. After the Cerise tarn the track follows a stony cwm to ultimate zigzags and the top (3¼ h.). On the Italian side a similarly good track descends without possible error into the Valle della Valletta, reaching a roadhead at the Pian della Casa (1743m.), and by this road to Terme di Valdieri (1¼ h. down to roadhead, 2¼ h. in ascent). Ital: Colle di Ciriegia.

Lac Nègre basin

COL DE SALESE   2031m.

See R.12, Adus hut. All excursions described below start from this col.
Using the Adus hut as a base adds 30 min. to all outward times; 45 min.
on inward times.

CIME DE ROGUE   2705m.

CIME DE PAGARI DE SALESE   2678m.

A long ridge running SW down to the Col de Salèse divides the Salèse
and Lac Nègre basins. A fine viewpoint for the Argentera massif, and
a recommended outing. Rogué = barren and rough.

South-West Ridge. A pleasant training walk, I-.

107.   From the carparking area at top of the Col a well marked track
follows the wooded then open ridge to the Pte.de Rogué (2435m.).
Continue along an undulating section called Serre de Rogué, then a
steady ascent to the Cime de Rogué (2 h.). Descend NE to the Baisse
de Rogué (2581m.) in 30 min. From here a track descends NW to the
Lacs de Fremamorte and the Camp Soubran path, overgrown in places,
leading back to the Col de Salèse. To continue, mount an easy scree
ridge to the Cime de Pagari in 20 min.(about 3 h. from Col). A further
continuation is possible to the Fremamorte pass and peak.

CAYRE DE ROGUE   2641m.

Impressive tower on a secondary ridge detached NW from the Cime de
Rogué. Several short rock climbs; easiest way (II) lies on facet above
and just L of gap on inner side of tower.

CIME DE FREMAMORTE   2730m.

COL DE FREMAMORTE   2615m.

108.   The col is a long disused military passage across the frontier.
The mtn. is almost certainly climbed more frequently from the Italian
side where a string of pretty lakes along a huge terrace is a popular
walk from the Valle della Valletta roadhead. From the French side,
as for R.112 to pt.2270m. where the jeep road in large blocks slants
L. A scree tip lies R (E); follow a track below this near rock pools and
continue under S side of the mtn. along edge of the hummocky Camp

Soubran area to a series of zigzags eventually rising N to the col. A track on the Italian side returns NW across scree below the SE ridge to reach the top shortly, I- (2½ h. from Salèse col).

CAYRE POUNCHU 2495m.

Prominent landmark beside the Lac Nègre outfall. From end of lake reach the foot of N ridge up a steep unpleasant clapier, narrowing to a gully of loose blocks at top. Follow crest in steps to the second of two shoulders (I+). Continue up a final step of 40m. with pitches of II, then a few m. of scrambling to summit (1 h.).

TETE SUD DES BRESSES 2824m.

109. Bresses are the hollows containing the mtn.'s namesake lakes. As for R.112 to pt.2270m. Go along the side path to the Soubran camp area for 150m. distance, then turn N on a small track winding up the grassy depression on E side of Cayre Pounchu to the first Bresses lake (2458m.). Continue R (ENE) across the flank of a large hillock then bear L to reach the second lake (2501m.). Go along its E shore then trend L of N up a grassy brow to join a track coming in from the L. Take this to the Collet des Bresses (2618m.) on the frontier ridge. Take L side of broad ridge to another depression. Now keep slightly L (W) with a broken track in scree and blocks up to a rock triangle forming a shoulder (junction with parallel Cayre des Bresses ridge). Continue along main ridge briefly to cairned summit, I- (3 h. from Salèse col). To reach the Tête N (2826m.) along the craggy ridge extending NNE involves poor rock and pitches of II, not recommended. To return by Lac Nègre, go back to the shoulder triangle then descend across the W flank of the mtn. on slabby ground with a good track, under the W facet, to reach a pt. near the Pas des Tablasses; then go straight down blocks, scree and grass to the Préfouns trail near pt.2479m. See the Tablasses mtn. below for further comments.

TETE DES TABLASSES NE.2855m. SW.2825m.

Oddly formed lop-sided mtn. of first importance in the Lac Nègre area. Extensive cliffs and good rock climbing on Italian side. Fine panorama. Tablasses are snow and screefield zones tilted as of a roof. Easily combined with the Tête S des Bresses.

<u>South Side Gully</u>. The easiest way, I-. Axe useful as snow remains to early autumn.

110. A fairly regular rockband cut by numerous gullies girdles the S

side of the mtn. at a level rising R-wards above the Préfouns col. At the last bend below the col on R.112 (2¼ h.) a track goes off R (NE) under a tower on the ridge above then crosses grass and scree below the rockband. After some 7 narrow gullies a broader opening appears and the track peters out. Go up this scree funnel to a slope of large blocks and mount this to grassy scree (snow) either to the saddle between the two summits or by trending R reach the NE top directly (45 min., 3 h. from Salèse col).

Traverse by South-West and South-East Ridges. A classic excursion, the sporting limit for experienced walkers, II-.

111. As for R.110. Having passed below the first ridge tower take the 3rd gully cutting rockband above. This one is narrow but wider than the first two, and distinctly shorter. Its immediate companion R is of similar appearance. Go up its earthy bed and exit L over easy broken rock to the ridge above its lower steepness. From a short narrow terrace on the Italian side move up to a gully cutting L side of ridge; climb the first step in it then traverse out R, round the crest. Work up a little R of crest to scree which is followed to the SW top. Descend stones into the saddle dividing the summits (splendid views of the Italian cliffs) and continue on similar ground to NE summit (1 h., 3¼ h. from Salèse)

Go down the broad SE ridge which soon becomes sharp and falls in short steps. Keep on the L side below crest along ledges and slabs and only return to ridge at a prominent gap near bottom. From here a direct descent to Lac Nègre is possible over an unpleasant clapier. Alternatively, commence traverse below the S side rockband and soon join the track in stones leading to the Préfouns col (R.110), much the most comfortable inward leg. Lastly, peak baggers can easily attain the Tête S des Bresses (q.v. above) by traversing below (S side) the rock turret standing between the last gap and the Pas des Tablasses; from latter col go up the NW ridge of the Bresses for a few min. to where a good track

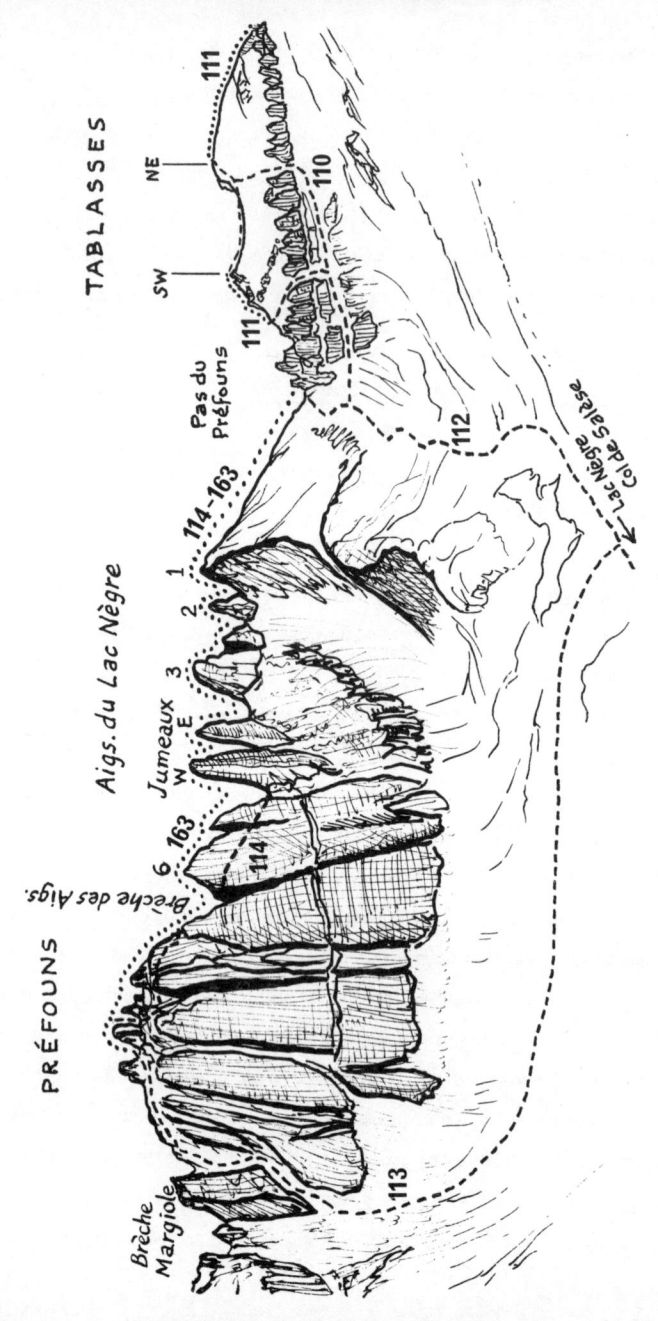

breaks R across its W facet, and rises through a slabby zone to the rock triangle shoulder near the summit, as in R.109. A descent of the latter route then completes an excellent round for returning to the Salèse col. From Tablasses summit thus to Salèse col, 3 h.

PAS DU PREFOUNS   2615m.

The chief col at the back of the Lac Nègre basin. In common with all passes hereabouts there are ruined military fortifications on the Italian side. Both sides are provided with a graded mule trail, I-. Préfouns refers to the profound rock defile so named on the Italian side.

112.   From the Col de Salèse descend 100m. on the W side to a jeep lane forking R; follow this to the ruined Agnellière barns (2053m.). A few steps before these turn R on to a small track ascending moderate slopes N in an open forest. This track is poor in places and does not always lie where the map indicates it. However it is difficult to lose if one remembers to stay on the higher ground on the L (W) of the stream flowing in the shallow forested valley to R. Eventually cross this stream R at an obvious place (2193m.) and ascend marshy terraces in zigzags bearing R to where the path rejoins the jeep road at 2270m. (This road is not driveable). Follow jeep road L among large blocks for 50m. then fork R up a narrower branch which forms the much improved mule trail (now possible for jeeps) ascending under W side of the Pounchu peak to reach broad platforms and beach at S end of Lac Nègre. Splendid outlook. Follow trail along E side of lake to pasture, hummocks and rocks beyond N end. A few zigzags lead to stagnant rock pools then a zone of huge boulders running into the clapier slope below the pass. The latter is ascended in long easy zigzags to top ($2\frac{1}{4}$ h. from Salèse col).

CAYRE DU PREFOUNS   2835m.
AIGUILLES DU LAC NEGRE

One of the most picturesque mtns. in the Mercantour Park, essentially complicated and on the Italian side sporning the magnificent Cresta Savoia. While the name Aigs. du Lac Nègre is often given to the entire pinnacled uplift of the mtn., the aigs. are strictly the first 6 or 7 big granite towers seen in profile to L as one approaches the Préfouns col; the last and most inward of these finishes at the Brèche des Aigs. du Lac Nègre. Above this gap the Préfouns proper culminates in 3 spikes, the central one being highest. The aigs. section offers good rock climbs, and a traverse of them is very traditional (IV). All this section can be turned but the continuation to the main summit is not without problems. The only rte. suitable for walking/scrambling parties is the SW ridge flank (see below). The large rock buttresses comprising the S face offer several good technical climbs.

First recorded ascent: V.de Cessole with A.Piacenza, J.Plent, 8 August,1899.

West-South-West Ridge Flank. Invariably used as the easiest descent from the mtn. In ascent the only possible way that walkers might try to reach the summit. The approach is tedious but the key section, a rising traverse across the S side of the WSW ridge, has interest. Frequent old waymarks, the rocks are smooth worn and are slippery in damp conditions; several short pitches of II. Good natural protection.

113. Start as for R.112. Leave the Préfouns col trail at the first big zigzag N of the lake, cross the inflow stream and ascend diagonally L up a grassy rock slope, turning a rockband R, to enter round a shoulder L the Margiole cwm below pt.2470m. From the 2nd zigzag access is equally simple but steeper, coming in behind pt.2470m. Traverse gradually NW into the bed and cross a clapier of massive rocks to scree slopes behind, rising to Brèche Margiole (2739m.). As this slope steepens a poor track can be found and followed close to the R side until about mid height in the Margiole couloir an obvious weakness appears in the R side. Ascend this weakness obliquely R with a better track to enter a narrow subsidiary gully coming down from the ridge above; go up gully to within 25m. of crest. A series of ledges, slabby ramps and short steps slant R across the S side, never far below crest. Start up steep broken rocks to R, crossing little ribs to follow this rising traverse

system. Several short vertical pull-ups between ledges and slabs, paint marked. Continue thus to pass below the W summit prong into a ridge gap and finish up a few m. of steep flaky rocks to the central prong and summit ($3\frac{1}{2}$ h. from Salèse col, $2\frac{1}{4}$ h. in descent).

<u>East Ridge Indirect</u>. One of the most recommended expeditions of its class in the park area; paradoxically an uneven scramble and confusing mixture of walking with intermittent sections of serious technical climbing. Not a feasible excursion for ramblers. Tricky route finding in poor visibility; in such conditions a party will be lucky to find the correct way in the upper part and must be prepared to climb additional pitches of III. Normally, pitches of II, one or two of III and one of III+. Magnificent rock scenery. First ascent: V.de Cessole with A. Ghigo, J.Plent, 27 November, 1899.

114. From the Pas du Préfouns (R.112) a faint track mounts a grass and rock slope to a slight shoulder just R (N) of the top of Gend.1. From here descend R in an earthy gully to the outer end of a long terrace covered with chaotic rocks, some the size of a house. Cross this terrace under the towers of Gend.2 & 3, then under two pointed ones, Les Jumeaux (4 & 5), to enter the gap immediately after these twins by a short rocky funnel (I+). Now move on to the L (S) side under Gend. 6 and slant over short rock steps (II-) to a ramp leading into a grassy gully. Go up a few m. and exit L by a little chimney (II-), then along a ledge and so down to the deep ridge gap and gully of the Brèche des Aigs. du Lac Nègre. All the latter aigs. have now been turned. A sub wall bordering the gully lies L of the crest line above. A slightly recessed wall section L of a chimney, itself L of crest line, is climbed by a thin crack system on good worn holds (15m., III with moves of III+), landing on a sloping terrace area. Wall direct further R = IV. Slant up L across terrace zone away from crest line and make a slightly

rising traverse L across a broad rock spur by short steps and ramps (II, sustained) to enter a gravelly gully. Climb its enclosing wall ahead at variable points. It is easy to start several m. lower down but steep rock soon forces one to climb half R into two corners 35m. above the gully bed. Climb these with a smooth slab between them (15m., III) to reach crest of this mass which comes down from the E forepeak before the trident summit. Now either traverse more or less horizontally, slightly up then down, over a zone of slabs (II, with one part III) for two rope lengths to enter the big gully coming down from the gap between the E and central summit prongs. Or, more easily, traverse over the slabs for 10m. only to a crack/groove going straight down to enter gully at a lower pt. Descend this "blind" crack on good holds for 35m. (II) into gully and reascend stony bed. From gap at the top climb a steep chimney straight above (II) to the flaky central prong ($2\frac{1}{4}$ h. from Préfouns col, $4\frac{1}{2}$ h. from col de Salèse).

TETE MARGIOLE 2852m.

Comparatively lofty summit retiring in a corner of the Lac Nègre basin, and the furthest pt. distant on the frontier that can be seen from the basin, hence the name, "limit". Rarely climbed.

POINTE GIEGN 2888m.

Massive roof-like mtn. on W side of Lac Nègre. Its gendarme studded NW ridge and the elongated SW wall offer numerous technical climbs on good granite. The name signifies a jutting jaw as might be seen on a skeleton with teeth intact. First recorded ascent: V. de Cessole with J.& J.B.Plent, 27 January, 1898.

115. <u>Normal Routes</u>, all starting from Col de Salèse. <u>South Ridge</u>, as for R.112 but go 200m. past the Agnellière huts before leaving the jeep road. Ascend N in a forest depression to rejoin road at a bend 300m. distance higher. Follow road round next sharp bend to a track on L going up to Lac Graveirette. Go round N shore and ascend

almost due W over stony slopes towards the Pte. Colombrons, reaching the ridge somewhat above this pt. Now follow the simple ridge with a steep headslope to summit, I- (2¾ h.).

East-South-East Ridge Flank. The quickest way down. In descent take the headslope for nearly 100m. to where a big gully develops below. Traverse L over scree towards the ESE ridge then go down steep scree and grass some 150m. distance from ridge. When a steep section appears below bear L towards ridge again and return R across a descending grassy ramp to a screefield below the steepness. At the bottom of this keep L along a broad spur and descend L after pt. 2425m. to the beach at the S end of Lac Nègre where R.112 is joined, I- (1¾ h. down to Salèse).

North-East Face Terraces. An interesting way for the adventurous, I. By R.112 leave main path at N end of Lac Nègre to contour round the lakeside into bottom of the Margiole cwm. A system of slanting and grassy/stony terraces crosses the immediate flank of the ESE ridge above from L to R. Turn a slabby rognon L in the cwm and go up bad scree to reach this system. Follow it across steep grassy buttresses and gullies to the last accessible gully before the summit line. Climb latter gully to exit on ridge above its last step from where the edge of the summit headslope is taken in a few min. to top (3½ h.).

From SW, Col de Fremamorte, L to R: Corno Stella, Argentera, Paganini, Nasta, Baus, Bastione.

Argentera chain

This massive spur is detached N from the frontier ridge at the Cime Guilié (R.105). The chain builds up in summit groups each more imposing than the last to culminate in the complex Argentera itself with several important satellites and wings.

CIMA DEL BROCAN 3054m.

Brocan = rocky. Rarely climbed. The shortest way is across the Col Guilié (R.19,20) to make a rising traverse over scree and snow across the wedge shaped W flank below the SSE ridge, to finish by a shallow gully reaching this ridge about 250m. distance from summit. Follow crest to a V gap below, which is reached by a steep staircase (25m., II). Avoid the vertical ridge step ahead by slanting R up a terrace/ramp for one rope length, then climb a headwall directly to summit (20m., II+) (2 h. from col). V.de Cessole with J.B. & J.Plent, 18 March,1896.

IL BASTIONE 3047m.

Quite distinctive rock peak, rarely visited. Normally climbed from Colle del (Pas) Brocan (2892m.) by the S ridge with an initial step then by W side of crest over a gap to turreted summit giving short but steep pitches of II. F.Mondini with G.Demichelis, 28 June,1898.

CIMA DEL BAUS 3067m.

A tent-like summit of abrupt rocks, hence its name, with big cliffs on S side. Rarely climbed but a noted viewpoint. Most easily attained from the Colle della Culatta (c.2950m.), the saddle between the mtn. and the Nasta, by NW ridge (I). V.de Cessole with J.B. & J.Plent, 23 January,1901.

CIMA DI NASTA 3108m.

An attractive, imposing rock peak whose couloirs generally hold snow throughout the season. An ice axe should be carried at all times. There is a NW shoulder or subsidiary peak (3100m.) and a SW one, but the true top is another little knob behind the former. Rock, gneiss, giving numerous first rate rock climbs. Nasta = shaft or stump. First ascent: D.W.Freshfield with F.Devouassoud, 27 September,1878 (mistaken for the Argentera). In winter: V.de Cessole with J.B. & J.

Plent, 18 February, 1896. The distant approach from France deters many ascents.

<u>South Couloir</u>. The ordinary rte., usually a snow climb. In icy conditions it may be better to take the SE ridge. II. Average angle, 40°.

116. The couloir rises above the Lago di Nasta and slants somewhat R in centre of the S face. From the Remondino hut reverse R.19 to the lake (45 min.). From Le Boréon to the same place, $5\frac{3}{4}$ h. Ascend to foot of couloir and traverse in from L along a gangway R (15 min.) to climb first in the bed then on R side to the summit ridge which is reached a few m. from the top (1 h., 2 h. from hut, 7 h. from Le Boréon).

<u>South-East Ridge</u>. The best descent route. II.

117. As for R.116. From the lake work up directly below S face to the Colletto della Forchetta (2950m.), a small saddle L of the triple turrets of the minor Forchetta buttress, to finish up a snow or scree gully, or take rocks on its R side. From the saddle climb the ridge over several short steep steps, keeping somewhat to the R (N) side (2 h. from Remondino hut).

CIMA PAGANINI   3051m.

A lesser twin for the Nasta, with a double summit, easily climbed by going up the big W couloir of the Colle di Nasta (2939m.) on steep scree, more pleasantly with frozen snow, then up the rocky S ridge (I). The continuation traverse is quite difficult. V.de Cessole with V.Bernart, J.Plent, 25 August, 1902.

MADRE DI DIO RIDGE

This pinnacled ridge extends WSW from Cima Genova (most southerly outlier of the Argentera) to which it is linked by Colletto Freshfield. The main summits are: Cima di Cessole (2915m.), Cima Maubert (2865m.), Madre di Dio (2800m.). Nearly all routes involve technical climbing. Note that map pt.2960m. is a misprint for 2860m. (Cima dei Camosci).

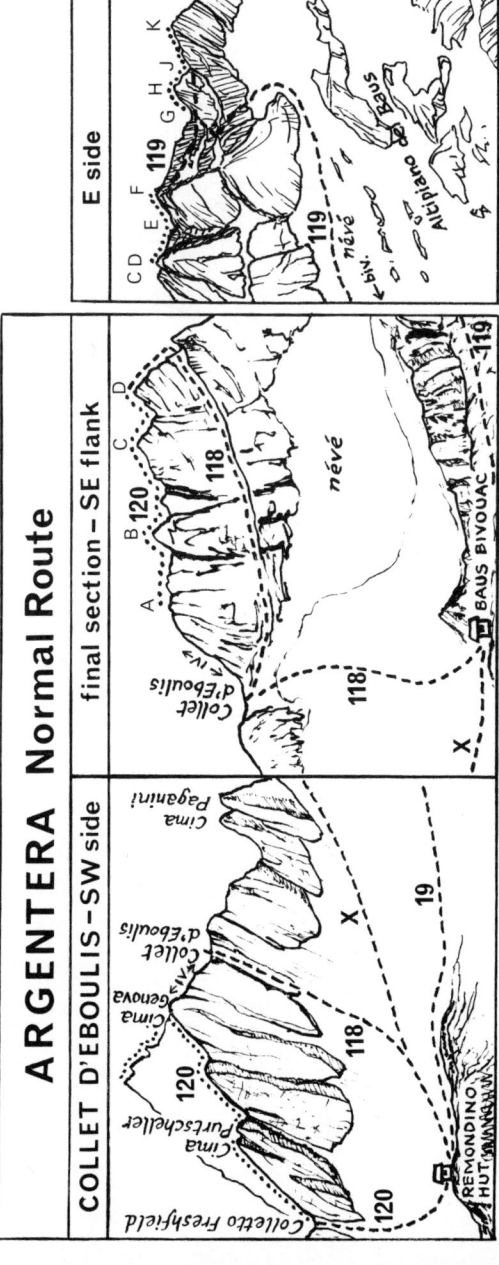

ARGENTERA Normal Route

COLLET D'EBOULIS – SW side | **final section – SE flank** | **E side**

Collet d'Eboulis = Passo dei Detriti

X = Remondino–Baus biv. connection over Colletto della Forchetta (2950m.), see notes in R. 117, 118.

A Cima Genova
B gendarme
C La Spalla
D S Peak
E Forcella
F N Peak
G Colletto Günther
H Gelas di Lourousa
J Colletto Coolidge
K Monte Stella

CIMA ARGENTERA   3297m.

The highest mtn. in the Maritime Alps is a long S-N ridge with complex spurs and buttresses on its W side; the summit is near the S end. There are four main tops and their traverse is highly recommended. The normal access pt. at S end of ridge is the Passo dei Detriti (3120m.), really a shoulder. Working N from here the following features can be identified: Cima Genova (3191m.), Forcella Genova (3170m.), La Spalla (3257m.), Cima Sud (3297m.), Forcella dell'Argentera, called simply the Forcella (3240m.), Cima Nord (3286m.), Colletto Günther (3190m.), Gelas di Lourousa (3261m.), Colletto Coolidge (3220m.) and lastly Monte Stella (3262m.). An important branch ridge forks NW from the Gelas top; it falls to a deep gap above which rises the famous Corno Stella, followed by a continuation in the Guides' Chain. Contained between this ridge and the main one is the great icy ravine called the Canalone di Lourousa. Argentera is the silvery mtn.

First ascent (by Lourousa couloir): W.A.B.Coolidge with C.Almer père et fils, 18 August, 1879. In winter: V.de Cessole with D.Martin, J.B. & J.Plent, 23 January, 1902.

<u>South-East Flank</u>. The most adventurous route of its class on a big mtn. in the Maritime Alps. Ice axe useful. Parties aiming to reach the top from Le Boréon in a day will find the going hard and long unless very fit. A projected new hut at the top of the Erps valley, in the Guilié cwm (R.19), should save $2\frac{1}{2}$ h. Easy and comfortable from the Remondino hut. All approach routes converge on the Passo dei Detriti. II-.

118. From the Remondino hut ascend to the rear on grassy rocks, scree and blocks slanting gradually L for 50m. then traverse L into the bed of the upper Assedras cwm. Go up this with large blocks and a few cairns into the NE corner where a scree/snow gully half L rises to the main ridge. A small track zigzags up its detestable scree for some distance; when it becomes poor move L on to the flanking broken buttress and ascend this to the top; Passo dei Detriti (2 h.). In descent, follow the couloir bed all the way down. Beware of rolling stones.

From Le Boréon take R.19 to the Nasta lake, then R.117 to the Colletto della Forchetta (6 h.). From this saddle follow a big ledge line more or less horizontally under the E side of the Nasta to the Colle di Nasta (2939m.). Now descend the E flank for 50m. to a zone of large blocks, then traverse scree and rocks NE under the cleft summit pile of the Paganini and above a rockband to the lower of two notches hereabouts in its E ridge. Continue the traverse along an exposed and interrupted grassy ledge line (II-) to a broad saddle in the main ridge beyond and N of the Paganini. Follow the ridge up a little facet to shoulder pt.3050m. and continue up the crest to the shoulder of the Passo dei Detriti ($1\frac{1}{2}$ h., $7\frac{1}{2}$ h. from Le Boréon).

From the Baus biv. hut go L across slabby rocks and climb a scree slope trending R into narrows leading up L into a snowy hanging cwm. Keep up the L side to reach the Passo dei Detriti, easy but steep and loose ($1\frac{1}{4}$ h.).

At the Passo, traverse R and slightly downwards under a large rock outcrop and contour round N to a long diagonal gangway slanting up gradually from L to R across the E wall of the main ridge under Cima Genova; follow this line, narrow and exposed in places, with an interruption formed by a step taken in descent over a rounded slab. Further along pass a scree gully rising towards the summit area, and near the top of the gangway climb a chimney/couloir with a chockstone to the E ridge of the mtn. About 30m. of scrambling remain to the S peak (45 min., $2\frac{3}{4}$ h. from Remondino, $8\frac{1}{4}$ h. from Le Boréon but possible with reasonable fitness in 7 h., 2 h. from Baus biv.).

Main Ridge Traverse (South-North). This is described from the main S peak to Mte. Stella. Normally you return the same way. (The first part of the ridge from the Passo dei Detriti over Cima Genova and La Spalla, to the S peak, has pitches of IV). Impressive views and situations, recommended, II.

119. From S peak go down a few m. R (NE) on easy rocks then bear L into an earthy gully in pale rock (I+) which leads down to grassy

ledges. Follow these N, narrow and erratic with short pitches (II), then trend upwards to reach the Forcella. From this gap traverse a short way L and climb steep rocks (II-) into a gully on W side of crest; follow this (I+) to rejoin crest a few m. from top of N peak (45 min.). Or by crest of main ridge above the Forcella, 3 short pitches of III.

From N peak descend a rocky slope NE for 50m. to a terrace line running along to Colletto Günther. From this gap the ridge can be climbed direct at grade II, or turned on the L (W) side by a ledge line to finish up a crack (II) at the summit of the Gelas di Lourousa (30-45 min.). From the Gelas top go down steeply with a turning movement R (E) halfway down (pitches of II) to Colletto Coolidge (15 min.). This gap is normally a snow/ice crest, being the head of the impressive Lourousa couloir. The Gelas summit can be avoided altogether, as most parties elect, by remaining on the terraces below the N peak and stopping just short of Colletto Günther. Continue the traverse line which remains good under latter gap and under E side of the Gelas without difficulty to enter the Coolidge gap. This traverse may be snow covered to late season (N peak to Coolidge gap, 30 min.). Now finally take a steep rock ridge direct (II) to the top of Mte. Stella (15 min.). Time: $1\frac{1}{2}$-2 h. according to route. Add 30 min. for return by same route.

The shortest way back to the Remondino hut is to descend from the terraces under the Günther gap by a zigzag line straight down E flank into a gully slanting L. At the bottom of this and its scree outflow slant R (SE) down a scree/snow hollow towards the ridge barrier whose first tier is marked by the Baus biv. hut (2696m.). Cross terraces below this tier and continue traversing at this level over scree and grassy bits under the Paganini to enter the cwm between the latter and the Nasta further S. Ascend this cwm over scree and blocks for 400m. to Colle di Nasta (2939m.), whence the snow/scree gully on its W side leads down to the Assedras cwm and the Remondino hut ($3\frac{1}{4}$ h.).

ARGENTERA W face

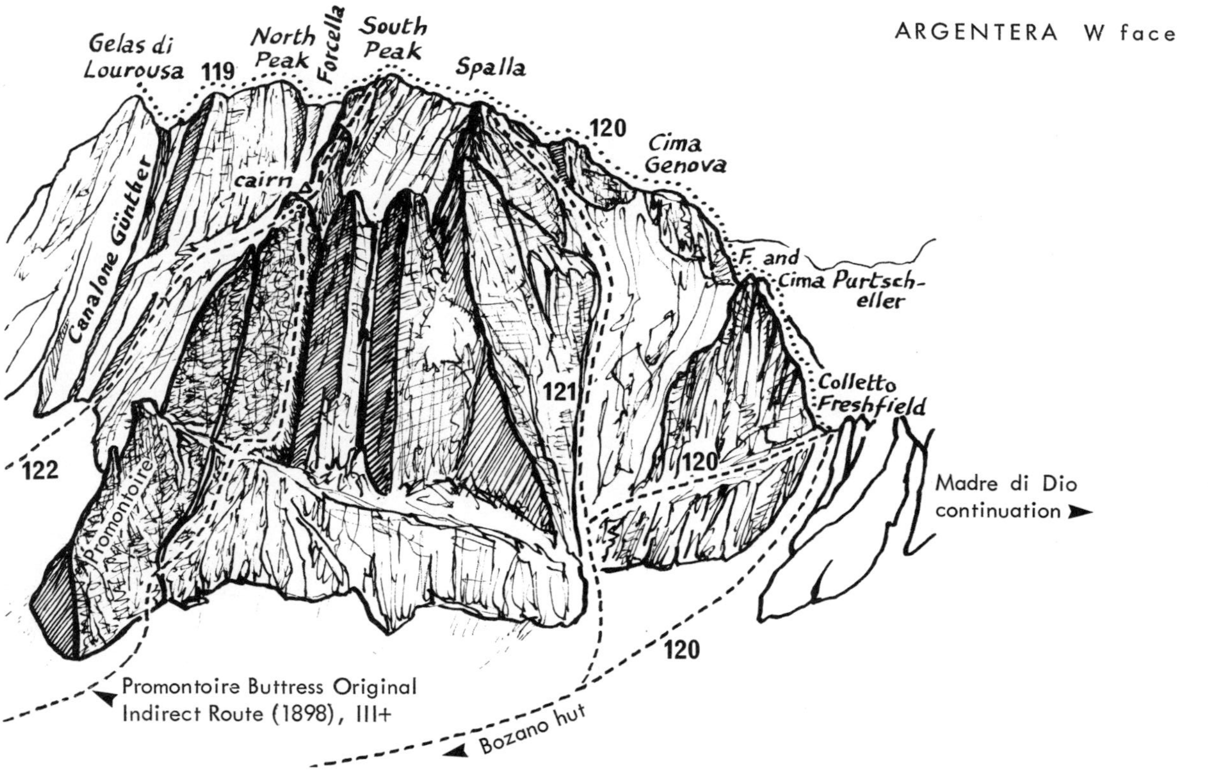

Gelas di Lourousa · North Peak · Forcella · South Peak · Spalla · Cima Genova · F. and Cima Purtscheller · Colletto Freshfield

119
120
121
122

cairn

Canalone Günther

M.te Promontoire

Promontoire Buttress Original Indirect Route (1898), III+
Bozano hut
Madre di Dio continuation

South Ridge. Up to Cima Genova the ridge is SW. The classic mountaineering way to the S peak, magnificent climbing, fairly serious, highly recommended, III. First ascent: A.Brofferio, V.Sigismondi, 24 June, 1908.

120. From the Remondino hut start as for R.118. From the cwm bed ascend rough ground to the foot of the SSW spur of Cima Genova and go up scree below its L side into a gully slanting R, up to Colletto Freshfield (2820m.) (1 h.). From the Bozano hut work S along a cairned water source track and continue S across a hollow under the Günther couloir and the Argentera W face. Go round base of the Promontoire buttress and lesser projections under the Argentera, and under a big ravine outfall from the face, up to foot of the snow/ice gully rising to the Freshfield col (1 h.). Climb this (crampons), stonefall possible, II (1-1½ h. for gully). To avoid gully there is a variation on the broken wall above L side of gully, as shown on diagram (II).

From col climb a short red wall, then the crest to a grey wall (III). At the top of this make a rising traverse 40m. L to a crack. Climb this (10m., III) to large blocks, then scramble R to top of shoulder called Cima Purtscheller (3040m.). On the L (N) side descend a short wall and reach the gap of Forcella Purtscheller. Continue up the crest in a fine position to Cima Genova (2½ h.). From here descend a short wall on the crest, then drop down on the R (E) side and traverse into Forcella Genova. Traverse a slab R to a ledge on the E side with a gendarme above. Either turn it on the R side into a gap, or from the turning movement climb it by a short steep wall (III), then descend to gap. Above is a smooth tapering slab; traverse R to a crack and go up this (II+), followed by a short descent to a stony terrace. From here another crack runs up to the Spalla then large blocks along the crest to S peak summit (45 min., 4¼ h. from Remondino hut).

Argentera from SE, seen between the Cayre (L) and Cime (R) de l'Agnel.

<u>Spalla (South-West) Wall</u>. One of the easiest routes from the Bozano hut, a fine mountaineering expedition with a serious air, on snow/ice, mixed terrain and fairly good rock. Several variations possible. Good route finding is needed in the upper part to keep the standard at grade III. 650m. V.de Cessole with A.Ghigo, J.Plent, 1 September,1908.

121. From the Bozano hut as for R.120 to the ravine outfall. Go up L side of this, hugging the wall forming the flank of a long buttress descending from the Spalla (by this buttress and its L side, III+). A steep snow/ice slope lies here which may be avoidable in a gutter at its L edge. Ascend to the entrance of a couloir rising to the Forcella Genova high above, between Cima Genova and the Spalla. Climb L of the main couloir into a rock gully cutting the narrow Spalla wall. According to conditions, either take its bed or rocks on the L or R sides, to emerge on steep mixed ground above. Ascend direct into a L branch of the main couloir which is followed until a rib on its L can be attained and followed to the Spalla summit. Then by a short blocky ridge to the S peak (5 h. from hut).

<u>West Face Diagonal Route</u>. The normal and most direct route from the Bozano hut, generally III with a pitch of IV. 700m. Serious mixed climbing. J.Brocardi, V.Paschetta with G.Ghigo, 26 August,1930.

122. From the Bozano hut ascend below the Corno Stella by a small track and cross a spur to a grassy saddle well seen from hut. Then go up a snowfield below the Gelas di Lourousa, followed by rocks L of a little waterfall to base of the Günther snow/ice couloir on R (1 h.). Its lower part is distinguished by a huge chimney formed in grey slabs and walls with chockstones. Ignore the couloir and climb a steep secondary gully up to the R. Turn a step by a chimney on L (II+), cross a ridge at the top of the gully and descend scree/snow to traverse a snow field poised at mid-height in the Forcella couloir which cuts the W face

from top to bottom. Cross snow with an open stream in its gutter to the far side which is closed by the Promontoire spur of the W face. At the level of the base of the upper Forcella couloir above, the flank of the Promontoire ahead is cut by two chimneys. Go into the lower R-hand one and climb it (II+) to the crest of the Promontoire at a small saddle and cairn. Continue up the fine ridge with pitches of III, the last with a yellow overhang which is turned R (IV). A short scramble remains to a hanging screefield (snow), leading to the main ridge just R (S) of the summit (5 h. from hut).

Note: The Günther couloir is the easiest way up on this side to the main ridge where R.119 can be joined. It is 600m. high and the route varies according to conditions, mostly a few short pitches of III-/III. The L side slabs and terraces are climbed in zigzags to mid-height, then the bed or the R edge to Colletto Günther at the top ($3\frac{1}{2}$ h. from hut).

123. <u>Canalone di Lourousa</u>. This enormous couloir gives the finest snow/ice climb in the region and was used by Coolidge for the first ascent of the mtn. Most of the upper part is at 45°, rising to 50° towards the top. 900m., III. Some stonefall danger; normally good snow to end June, afterwards getting progressively more icy. Crampons.

From the Varrone biv. hut (R.17) follow a small track in zigzags up the R side of the stream issuing from the Canalone. Keep to the R side up old moraine to a large terrace area of moraine hummocks and snow (fountain) under Piacenza and Ghigo (Guides' Chain), then move L to foot of couloir at c.2350m. Cross the bergschrund as far L as possible, ascend a snow groove then trend R before going straight up and keeping L in the line of three rock islets for 300m. A little higher, opposite the big gap which severs the Corno Stella from the parent mtn., the gully narrows and steepens to 45°. Climb keeping slightly L again all the way to a steep finish at Colletto Coolidge ($3-4\frac{1}{2}$ h., $4-5\frac{1}{2}$ h. from biv. hut). The main summits of the mtn. are now reached by R.119.

★

MONTE MATTO   3097m.

An isolated massif on N side of Terme di Valdieri. On this (S) side a series of ravines about 1500m. high run straight up to the summit ridge; tedious, rarely climbed and not recommended. This splendid group is nearly always approached from its N side, from the Sella lake and hut.

Here a small glacier and boiler plate hillocks come down at a moderate angle from a low relief and serrated summit ridge orientated NE-SW. The E peak (3088m.) is easy; the Central peak (3097m., not marked on map) requires a little rock climbing; more climbing for a continuation to the W peak = Cima Bobba (3079m.). First ascent, E peak: Capt. La Rocca, 1830. Central peak: W.A.B.Coolidge with C.Almer father and son, 14 August, 1879. In winter: V.de Cessole with A.Ghigo, G.Lovera, 26 February, 1911.

124. <u>Main Ridge Traverse</u>. A first rate scramble, recommended. Grade I-/I to E peak, II for the traverse. Axe useful.

From S.Anna di Valdieri follow the waymarked mule trail No.N4 up the R side of the Meris valley to the Dante-Livio Bianco hut (1917m.) above the E shore of the Sella lake (1882m.) (3 h.). Warden and restaurant service in summer.

From the hut take the mule trail W (N25) to the Lago Soprano della Sella (2329m.) (1 h.). Continue along another path S (N17, Colle di Valmiana) to a lesser L fork near pt.2456m. Take this obliquely L, winding up to the Lago del Matto tarns (2538m.). Go almost due E over rubble then a snow slope rising towards the W facet of the E peak. Go up this by its L side on scree to top (4 h. from hut).

For the traverse, descend a track in scree to the Forcella del Matto from where the ridge crest direct (II-) is taken on good rock to the Central peak (30 min.). In a few m. quit ridge by a small gully on S side, then traverse into next gap. From here follow crest over two small towers (II+) to the narrow col called Passo Cougné. Now traverse R into a chimney on the N side, climb this for a few m. then exit R below the next tower and traverse to the next gap. Follow the crest over two small red gendarmes to a small gap and continue to a cairn. Descend slabs to the last gap then the crest leading to the W peak (2 h.).

From the W peak descend a series of ledges and broken walls on N side, slanting L into a gully coming down behind a big gendarme further along the ridge. Exit from the gully keeping L (W) to reach a track on the Passo Cabrera (2780m.) (1 h.). Descend track on N side to join the Colle di Valmiana path on the outward leg near pt.2456m. (1¾ h., 9¼ h. for round trip).

High level touring routes

Two cross country treks can be made on the French side near the frontier ridge of the Mercantour Park region. On the Italian side the pattern of valleys and ridges works against a convenient touring route.

The long distance trekking route from Holland to the Mediterranean, GR5, skirts the SW edges of the Mercantour region. A variation, designated GR52, makes a huge detour starting from Valdeblore near St.Martin-Vésubie to follow the valleys and ridges closest to the finest scenery in the Maritime Alps. GR52 marks a great arc passing through the Salèse-Boréon basin into the head of the Fenestre valley, then crosses into the Gordolasque, Valmasque and Merveilles areas. It does not exit E to the Col de Tende road; instead the trail continues S along forested ridges to Sospel then Menton on the Riviera.

One of the recommended high level routes is the portion of GR52 extending in the reverse direction from the Merveilles to Valdeblore/St. Martin. The other is similar and parallel, working even more closely to the frontier ridge and consequently crosses rougher terrain and cols.

All adjoining major summits described previously in the guide can be reached easily from either route, sometimes in the course of day stages or by stop-overs and extra days spent at huts en route.

Recommended day stages and diversions, etc. are as follows. Route numbers are those given in this guide.

GR52 Route

Enter the region from St.Dalmas-de-Tende and go up the Minière valley (R.25) to the Merveilles hut. It is worth spending a day or two here, visiting the rock engravings and climbing Mt.Bego, Cime du Diable, or more ambitiously the Gd.Capelet. Continue to the Nice hut by R.3; Cime Chaminèye is easily climbed by a short diversion after dumping sacs near the upper Niré lakes. At the Nice hut a day or two can be taken to climb Mt.Clapier and the Maledie; both are possible in the same day. From the Nice hut continue by R.2 to the Madone; possible to climb either Cayre/Mt.Colomb or Mt.Ponset en route by leaving sacs at the Pas du Mt.Colomb. At the Madone a stay of two or three days could be taken for climbing the Gélas, St.Robert, Ponset or Neiglier. The next day stage goes from the Madone to the Cougourde hut (R.9), the latter actually a variation because GR52 avoids the hut by descending directly to the Peyrestrèche chalet. At the Cougourde hut a choice of first rate summits will delay the peak bagger, among them the Cougourde itself, the two Agnel peaks, the Ruine or Guilié.

From the Cougourde hut GR52 follows R.11 only to the Peyrestrèche bridge at 1838m. Here a forestry path forks R in the descent direction and contours slopes on the N side of the Boréon valley to join the Col de Salèse road above Le Boréon hamlet. This particular section is a popular nature trail for day visitors and is well marked throughout, and on map. A descent to Le Boréon hamlet can be made in 45 min. The trail continues up the unmade Col de Salèse road, avoiding wide bends as you wish, to the pass at the top. Camping apart, here it is necessary to stop overnight at the Adus hut (R.12, q.v. for keys, etc.). A keen walking party will want to stay here a day or two to tackle one of the summits round the Lac Nègre basin.

The last day stage goes from the Adus hut, over the Col de Salèse, down the road on the W side to the Collet huts (1842m.), from where the trail goes up the Barn valley S to the Col du Barn (2452m.) and across a plateau of tarns to the Col de Veillos (2194m.) to enter Valdeblore (St.Dalmas) below. Hotels, pensions, shops, etc. The road over Col St.Martin to St.Martin-Vésubie has a local bus service, or parties can walk there in a short day.

The entire route without summit diversions and other stop-overs or off days is occupied by 7 day stages. The Madone and Le Boréon are the only points where a walking party can use public transport to descend and replenish food supplies, etc. without losing more than half a day - by visiting St.Martin.

Classic High Level Route

Originally a tour for climbing parties making a ten-day visit to the area and wanting to ascend the main peaks without interruption.

Enter the region from St.Dalmas-de-Tende and go up the Castérine valley to the Valmasque hut (R.25,26,27). From here it is much less convenient to visit the Merveilles engravings, except by devoting a whole day to it. The Fontanalbe engravings can be visited by breaking the journey at Castérine hamlet (R.26). The next stage crosses the Pas de la Fous to the Nice hut (R.4) with the possibility (normal) of climbing Mt.Clapier on the way. Other diversions from the Nice hut as noted above. Now you either follow the GR52 way over the Pas du Mt.Colomb (R.2), or take the tougher original way which is to reach the Madone by first climbing the Gélas (R.62,68,67 in ascent, and 67 in descent). Sacs must be carried all the way to the foot of the final East Couloir of the mtn. Then the short easy stage from the Madone to the Cougourde hut by R.9.

The hard stages now occur as a big detour N to climb the Argentera. This can be done in a day and back from the Cougourde hut but it is not likely that a party unfamiliar with the terrain will find its way in darkness. A daylight departure could also mean returning after nightfall. Normally you go in daylight to the Remondino hut (R.20,19), preferably on a Friday, Saturday or Sunday when the hut will be open, ascend the Argentera next day and return the same day to the Cougourde hut, or more directly to Le Boréon by following R.19 throughout. Naturally, this important detour to the Argentera can be missed out.

Thereafter as for GR52 to the Adus hut for scrambles or climbs in the Lac Nègre basin.

Selected technical rock climbs

Generally refer to same mtns. in main part of guide for descent routes.

MALEDIE

130. <u>South-West Face, Super Direct</u>. The pillar directly beneath the summit, 200m.,V+. D.L.Bianco, E.Buscaglione, G.Ellena, 20 August,1946. Approach as for R.60, where the diagonal goes R. At foot of pillar climb vertical rock for 8m. to a narrow, slightly overhanging chimney; go up this with pegs. Two easier pitches lead to an impressive pitch between a black crack on L and the Meade couloir on R. Continue up short cracks for 60m. then climb a series of exposed slabs (peg belays) to below a smooth red wall 8m. high. Descend 10m. and follow a short gangway on R to a chimney/crack. Make a long stride to a steeply sloping ledge leading to ridge 20m.L of summit (4 h.).

131. <u>SW Face, Meade's Direct</u>. The couloir to R of the Super Direct, not at all obvious at first. Fine and very steep in lower part, 200m., IV. C.F.Meade with P.Blanc, 30 September,1910. Ascend the R.60 diagonal for 35m. (one delicate step,II). Now climb vertically above gangway line on good rock towards a big scoop in upper part of a steep reddish wall. Attain delicately a grassy terrace in middle of the scoop (40m.,III,III+). Go a few m.R, then move up directly until the scoop peters out. Now climb a couloir and a chimney. Pass L of an obvious roof (visible from foot of wall) and so to foot of red vertical wall (3 rope lengths, III & III+, step of IV, poor rock). The couloir becomes less obvious and trends slightly R below the red wall. Then two more rope lengths, the second exposed on the edge of a rock blade, to exit a few m. from summit (III+,II,III) (2½ h.).

CAYRE COLOMB

132. <u>East Face Direct</u>. A little classic, easily followed, with good rock. Found on steep triangular face below SE summit, 200m.,IV/V-. G.& N.Dufour and party, 18 September,1956. From the Madone or Nice huts by R.2. About 50m. below E side of Pas du Mt.Colomb cross grass and rubble to foot of face (2¼ h.). Start 10m.L of lowest point, climb easy rocks (II) to foot of slabs, and go up these towards an overhanging chimney L (50m.,III). Traverse R a short way, climb a steep slab and exit R. Return L and ascend a short gully (15m.,IV). Above

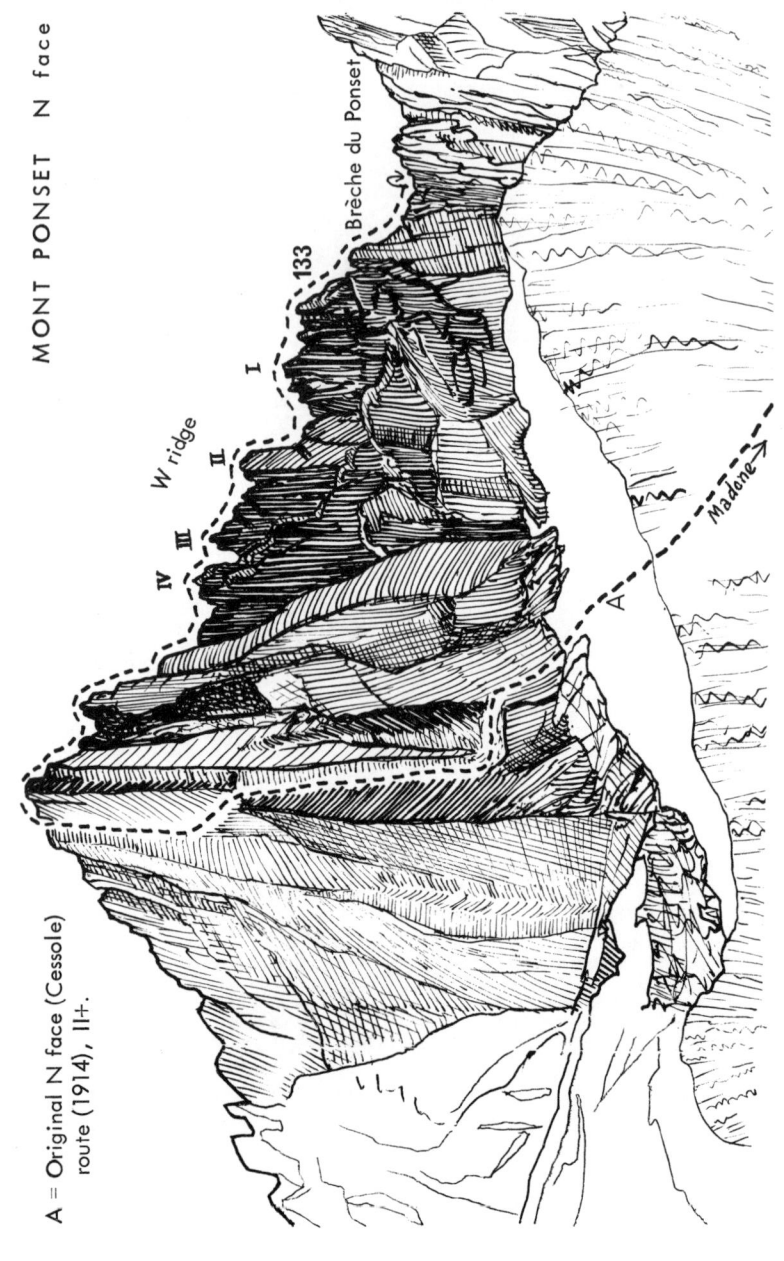

A = Original N face (Cessole) route (1914), II+.

this climb a vertical wall direct on good holds to small stance and a good belay (20m.,IV). A long crack slanting R leads to a ridge (30m. IV+). Climb a few m. on ridge then traverse L along a ledge. Now a steep move up a wall (V-); then move R and continue R of the ridge (III). Rejoin ridge and follow to top (2½ h.).

PONSET

133. <u>West Ridge</u>. One of the great classic climbs of the French zone. The ridge has 4 big gendarmes and generally sound rock, delicate and exposed. Considerable variation is possible. 300m., IV+ by the easiest way. Descended in 1923. Climbed indirect by M.Laporte, G.& J. Vernet, 24 August,1930. All the gendarmes had been climbed direct by 1935. From the Madone by R.80 to near foot of W face. Work L and climb steep grassy rock (II) to the R-hand of twin gaps separated by a rock finger at foot of W ridge (Brèche du Ponset, 1¾ h.).

Start up L side of ridge, then 2 short slabs to crest, and a dièdre on R (50m.,IV,IV+,IV,IV+). Continue by crest over Gend.1 (20m.,III) to next gap (III) and up to a shoulder below Gend.2 (IV-). A slab L,an awkward step R to a dièdre and up this to near crest. In 5m. reach crest and follow to top of Gend.2 (30m.,IV & V-,peg). Follow crest for 15m.(III) then steeply to a slab on R (IV) reaching top of Gend.3 (20m.,IV). Traverse L into next gap. Now two possibilities. Either a smooth slab followed by a leaning groove and a short couloir to a shoulder (20m.,V,pegs); or, easier, descend 2m. from gap and traverse L to the buttress rising to the shoulder (25m.,IV & IV+). Now follow crest to top of Gend.4 (20m.,IV-). Abseil 5m. to next gap and climb slabs to a shoulder platform below final tower. Descend 3m.R to where a slab leads into a chimney and follow it to top (50m. III,IV,III) (4 h. from ridge gap).

134. <u>North Face</u>. A large and impressive face divided by a prominent pillar/spur falling from the summit, which is taken by the 1951 Dalou-Savin rte. (250m.,IV+). Either side of this are routes of II/III.

135. <u>East Face</u>. A triangular face S of the Pas du Mt.Colomb, and corresponding almost exactly with the Cayre Colomb one N of the col. A very steep, classic climb, 200m., IV+/V. Smooth, compact rock. Mlle.F.Cravoisier, M.Dufranc, 14 May,1961. From the Madone by R.2 to final scree/snow slope under the Pas. Slant somewhat R and reach a ridge gap 50m.R (S) and above main col. Climb a wall to R (5m.,II) to a platform, from where a grassy terrace slants down under the E face. Start from this terrace some 50m. from lowest point of

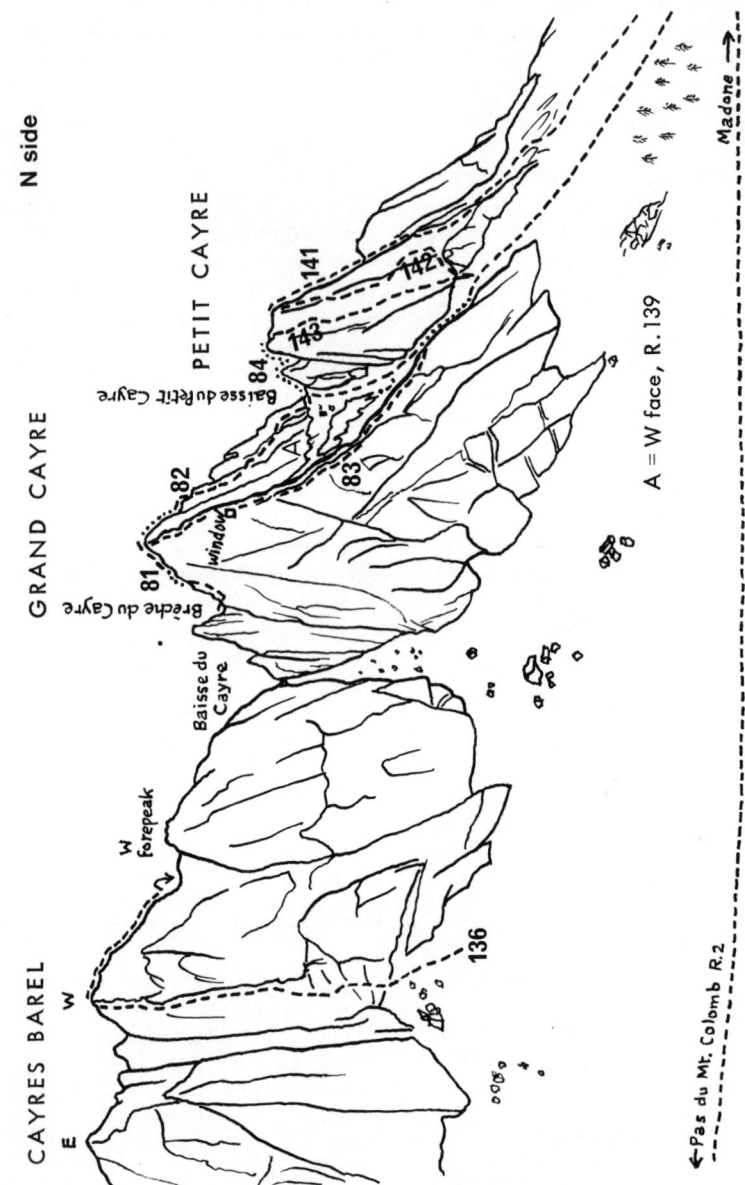

face, R of an inlet (2¼ h.). From Nice hut by R.2 to below main col, then a scramble L.

Start at cairn, where slabs of III and IV go up L. Avoid a steep part by a move L (V-). The open corner above has a slab on its L and a very steep wall (IV,V-) leading to a platform. Attain a dièdre from the R and climb its L wall (IV,V). Now take parallel grooves, first the R, then the L, and finally return to R one. A steep wall L gives access to a big ledge (IV+,V). The top of the face is a little higher, and the summit is 20 min. away along the E ridge (2½ h.).

CAYRES BAREL W PEAK 2600m.

136. <u>North-West Buttress</u>. A double rock peak (E. 2626m.) forming first part of extension from Ponset W ridge (main ridge traverse, III). A good climb, 300m., V in middle section, then IV. J.Chevaillot, G.Demenge, P.Gastaldi, E.Isch-Wall, 16 June,1957.

From the Madone by R.2 into the Mt.Colomb valley and ascend to R towards the couloir between the two Cayres Barel (1 h.). Start R of couloir and climb slabs to a ledge (40m.,IV,move of V). Move L round the edge and climb a dièdre then a cracked wall to a big ledge (IV+, moves of V, peg). Climb another dièdre and an overhanging crack; resting place on R (V, peg). Continue to a ledge of blocks; now take a wall on L and a reddish overhanging groove. Traverse L and rejoin the ridge by black slabs (V & V+, pegs). Follow crest to a gap and continue in a dièdre L of crest (IV). Finally by ridge to top (IV/IV+) (5½ h.).
Descend by W ridge, first on N then on S side, to gap between the W summit and a forepeak. From gap descend S couloir and return to Madone by the Ponset cwm.

GRAND CAYRE

Together with the Petit, a rock playground now covered with technical climbs, very popular because of proximity to the Madone.

137. <u>South (Red Tower) Buttress Original</u>. Not very sustained, 200m., V. L.Castelli, G.Demenge, G.Dufour, 21 February,1955. Approach from the Madone in 1 h. to obvious place at L side of S face. From the base ascend slabs to climb a steep step (IV,IV+). Then a wide crack to a big ledge R. A steep crack (IV,move of V, peg) leads to slabs on the crest. Grassy rocks (II), a gap, a little gendarme avoided L, a steep wall (IV) and more slabs lead to foot of the Red Tower. Climb an over-

hanging crack slanting R on to slabs and ascend these diagonally L to another ledge leading L (V- & IV+, peg). Descend 3m. L to climb a long chimney/crack (30m., IV-); finish via a platform and the crest at top of Red Tower (IV & IV+). Descend R to a gap and reascend grass gullies and rock steps to summit ($2\frac{1}{2}$ h.).

138. South-South-West (Windy) Ridge. 250m., IV+. J.Chabrier, G. & N.Dufour, October,1957. Below the S Buttress, start by a traverse in L on a grass terrace 30m. above and R of the ridge toe. The ridge flanks R side of the couloir running up to gap between the Gd. and Petit Cayres.

Ascend 25m.beside light grey rocks in the back of a dièdre, then a traverse L into it (30m., III then IV). A chimney leads to a gap (25m. IV+, II, IV+). Climb the narrow ridge face towards a tree which is reached from the R. Now a rising traverse R for 8m. to a platform (20m., IV). Climb a slab on its L for 4m.(peg) then traverse L to a rib, trending slightly L to a final slab and the ridge (35m., IV, one move V-, IV). Follow ridge to top of a gendarme (50m., II,III). Descend crest to a gap (20m., IV- for first 5m.). A buttress then a crack on L lead to ridge (20m., III+). From far end of a terrace on L, climb a wall to top of a gendarme (10m., move of V, IV+ then IV). Descend to a gap (8m., III+). A gully crack (30m., III) and then 2 pitches of II lead to top ($2\frac{1}{2}$ h.).

139. West Face. One of the best climbs on the mtn., slightly marred by poor rock at the beginning. Sustained, 200m., V+. Mlle.F. Cravoisier, G.Demenge, M.Dufranc, 19 May, 1957. Approach as for R.2,83 and ascend the couloir between the Gd. and Petit until steep broken rock on the L can be climbed to foot of the face (1 h.).

Awkward broken slabs, trending slightly L, lead to below overhangs (18m., IV). Climb steeply on R to enter a niche, then traverse a weakness R on delicate tilted slabs until cracked slabs above can be climbed direct to a ledge (35m., V, V+, IV, pegs). Continue direct at first, then trend L; surmount an overhang and follow a dièdre to where a wall L leads to a tree (35m., IV, IV+, V, sustained, pegs). Traverse R and climb a big groove, finishing over a overhang into a chimney. Ascend chimney to quit it by ledges L to a tree (IV,V & V+, pegs). Slabs of IV lead to top (4 h.).

PETIT CAYRE

140. South Ridge. A good and reasonably continuous climb, 150m., IV+. E.Isch-Wall, R.Marty, 30 June,1957. Approach as for the Gd.

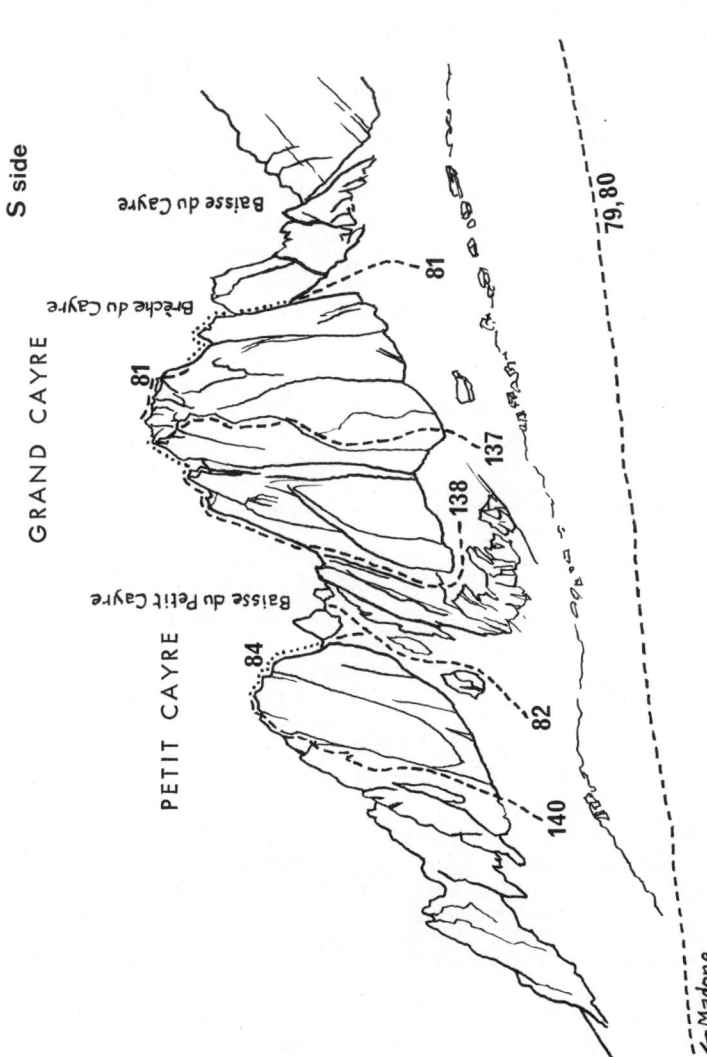

Cayre S Buttress and SSW Ridge, and start well below these (1 h.) up grassy rocks L of the crest line for 30m. A break leads R, then a slab and crack near the crest line reaches a gap (III+). Now a steep pitch to a good platform and tree; then 3 pitches of IV on the ridge to easy ground and top of first tower. Abseil 15m. to gap below and climb a bit L of crest up a cracked step to top of next gendarme (IV+, pegs). After the next gap take an open groove to top (III+) (2 h.).

141. West Buttress. A fine sustained route, 200m., IV+, one pitch V+. J.-L.Otto-Bruc, P.Roux, 1961. Approach as for R.2,83 and go up to buttress on R of big groove coming down from the NW ridge (45 min.). Ascend crest and turn a tower on L (III,IV-). Take next step on the L, and when it steepens return R by a slab. On the crest line a leaning wall (IV+,V+, pegs) and slabs (IV,IV+) lead to the upper part of the NW ridge (2 h.).

142. North-West Ridge. A first rate climb, 190m., V, on ridge that flanks N couloir of the Baisse. Steep, on excellent rock, which is however covered with lichen. J.Chabrier, F.Cravoisier; N.Dufour, C.Barillier, J.Botton, G.Dufour, 16 September,1956. Approach as for R.2,83, reaching a shoulder at foot of the ridge from the L ($\frac{3}{4}$ h.).

Traverse horizontally R and trend in the direction of the L-hand of two dièdres (20m., IV & III). Climb dièdre using two cracks, traverse R and exit by a layback (28m., IV, 2 moves of V, peg). Climb to below an overhang on R, then traverse L across the wall to a crack which is followed to the ridge (20m.,IV then III). Climb ridge somewhat on R, then cross the edge L to a crack in the back of a leaning groove. Go up this to a line of overhangs. Traverse R and pull up to a good platform - an intimidating pitch (25m., V then IV+, pegs). Climb a wall and a yellow flake, then traverse R across a rock corner. A short dièdre leads to a platform on L (20m.,IV+ then V, pegs). Climb a steep groove and exit R (25m., V- then III, peg). Another 40m. of II leads to top ($2\frac{1}{2}$ h.).

143. North Face (Right-Hand Route). A vertical climb on excellent but lichen covered rock, 180m., V+, sustained. G.Dufour, M.Jaubert, 26 May,1958. The start adjoins the NW ridge, to its L, at the centre foot of the face, with the Baisse couloir further L. Ascend 4m. in centre of face and traverse horizontally R to a detached block (20m. III). Mount block and climb cracked wall above for 20m., trending L over a bulge and slab, to finish delicately; continue to a stance (28m. V & V+, pegs). Trend R then return L, cross a wall to the L and go up an overhanging wall into a vague chimney which is climbed to an exit R on to a steep delicate wall. Climb this trending L to a stance (30m.

III,V,V+, pegs). Climb cracks to an overhang, surmount it, then traverse R to a stance at foot of a crack (20m., IV+,V+, peg). Climb crack to an overhang and surmount on L. Mantelshelf on a little ledge, continue up wall trending L and pass another overhang on L (30m., IV+ & V, pegs, sustained). Follow a ledge line rising L (20m.,III) and go up a slightly overhanging groove (V-) to a ledge. A crack to R (IV) leads to top (3 h.).
The more difficult Left-Hand (Rafaelli) Route (VI-) starts up an S-shaped crack L of the R-hand start.

NEIGLIER

This mtn. has several average interest climbs on its NNW face, some quite difficult and developed in the late 1970s.

POINTE ANDRE

144. <u>North Face</u>. Generally, see R.86. The best route on this face takes a big dièdre L of the edge of a gully falling from gap to the R (W) of main summit. The central section is well sustained and reminds of the E buttress of Clogwyn du'r Arddu. 200m., V. J.Botton, G.& N.Dufour, H.Petit-Jean, 17 July,1960.

Approach by R.79 to the Ponset lakes and ascend to foot of face (1¾ h.). Scramble 100m. to a narrow ledge running across and up to foot of the dièdre (II). Avoid the overhanging start by a steep wall on its L then climb the corner crack to a terrace (IV+,V,pegs). Climb another wall and return to corner at the level of a bulge, moving up to another big ledge (V & V+, pegs). Follow the dièdre, and take a little overhang and a crack with a jammed block (IV & V,peg). Now more easily and bear L to main ridge above, to follow this to top (3 h.).
The gullies either side below Brèche André are steep and unpleasant, but the S one is marginally more comfortable. In descent a jammed block pitch is turned L (II), and at the bottom follow down the Prals valley (R.87) to return to the Madone.

145. <u>South Buttress</u>. A good climb on the ridge bounding S face on L. 150m., IV+. Mme.Lippman, G.Demenge, J.Vernet, 31 March, 1957. By R.86 to the Baisse de Cinq Lacs. On the S side take a tiny track along the foot of rocks below the W ridge to base of the buttress (1¾ h.). Ascend a hollow and traverse R, then straight up a steep wall and dièdre to a shoulder (50m., IV & IV+). Easy climbing in a grassy weakness L of crest until a dièdre on its R can be entered and climbed (move of V-, then IV). The next section is IV to a traverse

R and a 20m. wall (IV). Now easily to top (2 h.).
On the S face to R is another good, short climb, 150m., V+, following a dièdre system just R of centre line up the face.

COUGOURDE

This magnificent rock spur provides the most accessible and greatest concentration of excellent rock climbs in the Mercantour Park. See also main entry in guide and R.96,97.

146. <u>South Couloir of Gap 2-3</u>. A useful way up to main ridge and a quick descent for parties returning from climbs on Peaks 3 & 4. II+, cairned. From the gap descend couloir and leave it after 100m. where it widens and bends R. At this pt. it is divided by a large gendarme. Exit L beside a cairn to gain a grassy shoulder a few m. L(E). Go down a 3m. slab to a ledge leading L in 5m. round to a gap. Now descend a steep 6m. step in a chimney (II+). Facing outwards, keeping going L along cracked slabs, using ledge in the middle (20m.). Go up 3m. steeply to a continuation grassy gangway R which is followed to a descent in a 25m. chimney (II+). So to a terrace ledge running L to foot of couloir below Gap 1-2, where normal route track R.96 is joined, 35 min. down, 1 h. up.

Peak 4, South Flank

All climbs on this side can be reached from the Cougourde hut in 1¾ h. or less by R.96.

147. <u>Peak 4, South Couloir</u>. Cutting R side of S face above the track, a strenuous and sustained section of 50m. starts this good climb, 220m., V, with a pitch of VI. K.Gurékian, M.Lenoir, 16 October, 1947. Climb the deep chimney/gully, avoiding the first overhang either in the bed or on wall to L (V-). The wall L of a second overhang is IV+, and a third overhang in the bed provides the crux (VI, peg). Difficulties now ease, trending R up to a shoulder. Continue direct and soon trend R again to top (3½ h.).

148. <u>Peak 4, Yellow (South) Wall</u>. A very steep and mainly free climb, one of the best of the more difficult rtes. hereabouts. 250m., V+. F.Cravoisier, G.Demenge, M.Dufranc, E.Isch-Wall, 29 September, 1957. Start in centre of wall, about 50m. R of balcony under SW ridge (track). 30m. of slabs trending R (III) are followed by a dièdre obliquely R to a ledge (25m., IV+). A short overhanging crack on R (V-, peg) is climbed to a ledge of blocks. Move L and continue L on flaky holds (15m., IV,V,peg) and a little L take another dièdre

(25m., V, V+, pegs). Traverse R then straight up two overhanging walls with cracks (25m., V-, A1, V+, pegs) to a line of ledges. Climb slanting R into top part of a dièdre (25m., IV), then by blocks R and a steep and awkward chimney (IV+) to shoulder on SW ridge. Finish up ridge (4½h.).

149. <u>Peak 4, South Wall Direct</u>. A splendid, sustained climb of 250m. V+. Takes Yellow Wall for 20m. then bears L to continue in a very direct line. F.Ruggeri, D.Ughetto, 14 August, 1966.

150. <u>South Corner</u>. The edge between the grey-brown and yellowish walls gives a sustained route, 250m., V. Numerous pegs.

151. <u>South-West Ridge</u>. A fine, classic and very popular climb of 300m., IV-. P.de Thiersant, P.Rouyer, P.Tordo, R.Tourmayeff and J. de Villeroy, 7 July, 1927. From the balcony shoulder (track) make a traverse L into large open corner (40m., II). Descend a little and continue traversing L, later upwards to foot of a crack in a corner hidden beyond the broad ridge line (30m., IV, II, IV). Big peg belay. Climb the crack (III, moves of IV-) with a stance halfway, then slabs and a short steep chimney (III+, IV-). The ridge lies back a little and slabs just L of the crest (III) lead up to a short wall (IV). This lands on an enormous boulder strewn terrace, the shoulder. Climb a crack near edge of the ridge (III) and follow edge to top (3 h.).

Peak 4, West Face

The impressive frontal rock wall, cut towards L side by a chimney/gully rising to Gap 3-4. Not the same approach as for S face rtes.

<u>West Face Dièdres Route</u>. A fairly sustained climb, 400m., V/V+. Approached as for R.97, latterly keeping R by a grass tongue R of a rock band (1 h.). The dièdre line in R-hand part of face (4 h.).

<u>West Face Overhangs Route</u>. Another good climb, 400m., V, with some V+/VI. Starts 20m. L of Dièdres Route and pursues a quite direct line (5 h.).

152. <u>Central (WNW) Pillar</u>. The pillar situated R of the so-called Central Couloir, in fact found towards L side of W face here formed jointly by Peaks 3 & 4. The couloir rises to Gap 3-4. A fine sustained climb with a big groove in its lower part. 425m., V. E.Isch-Wall, G.Demenge, J.-L.Martinoty, 3 August, 1962. Approach as for R.97 (1 h.).

A couloir on the R, just L of rockband at foot of wall. Climb it for 20m. then a crack/dièdre on L to top of a tower (50m., IV, move of V,

peg). Climb a wall/slab (V+ then IV+, peg) to re-enter dièdre/crack.
Follow it for 4 rope lengths, sometimes in the bed, sometimes on the L
slab (IV+, various moves V, sustained, pegs) and exit R by a chimney
(IV-). Cross the ledge of Z Climb (R.97) and 10m. R climb a red slab
to below a comma shaped roof (IV+). Traverse 5m. L to join crest of
pillar 10m. higher (V, pegs). Follow it for 30m. (IV) then an easier bit
of 20m. to foot of final wall. Climb 20m. by a cracked slab, step R
and get into a niche; exit rising 7m. L to crest (V, pegs). Above take
a narrow chimney (IV+, peg), then the edge leads to top ($5\frac{1}{2}$ h.).

Central Couloir. Uses the L crack of couloir coming down from Gap
3-4. 400m., mainly IV, a few pitches of V.

153. Peak 3, North Ridge (Dufranc Route). An excellent and satis-
fying climb, 250m., plus the terminal ridge, V. Direct start: Mme.
Demenge, G. Demenge, F. Ruggeri, 28 September, 1958. Approach as
for R.97. Round the promontory of Cairn Jeannel at L side of W face
is a large triangular wall rising to Peak 3. Its L-hand side is bounded
by the N ridge.

Climb the obvious dièdre coming down from a little shoulder on the N
ridge (120m., var. pitches, IV & V). Now a thin crack (V, pegs) leads
to a deep, exposed chimney (V+), and an overhang taken on the L (V+
peg). Continue up to L (IV+) to another overhang, again passed on L
(V+). A chimney opening out into a groove leads to a ledge at small
gap. Follow ridge to top of Peak 3 (III) ($3\frac{1}{2}$ h.).

154. Peak 3, North Ridge (Gurékian Route). A nice sustained climb,
170m. to terminal ridge, V. Mlle. R. Imbert, C. Ferretti, K. Gurékian,
6 October, 1946. Start at L side of broad buttress foot, in entrance to
R-hand branch of Y couloir going up to Gap 2-3. Take a weakness
rising to a small conspicuous shoulder on R. Do not go all the way up
to shoulder; instead climb vertically (III), then by a break to a platform
on edge of ridge (IV). A steep bit (IV) and a steep slanting line up to
L (V, peg) lead to a nice ledge overlooking R branch of the Y couloir.
Traverse 2m. R, then go directly over an overhang (V & V+, peg). Now
continue bearing R for 20m. (IV-) and avoid a corner R. Return L on
bad rock (III+) and climb a vague couloir (IV). Continue slightly L
to ridge, reached at pt. where its angle eases (III). Follow the narrow
crest to top ($3\frac{1}{4}$ h.).

Peak 2, North Ridge. The ridge between the branches of the Y couloir
gives a good climb, 220m., V-.

Peak 1, North Ridge. An interesting climb, 250m., IV.

COUGOURDE

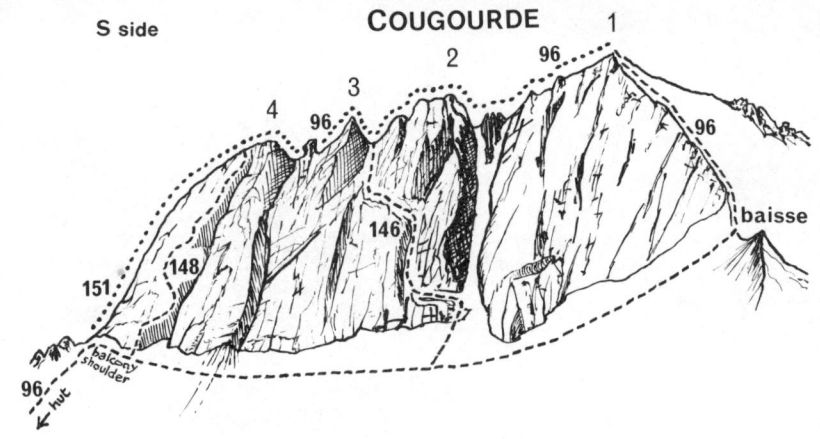

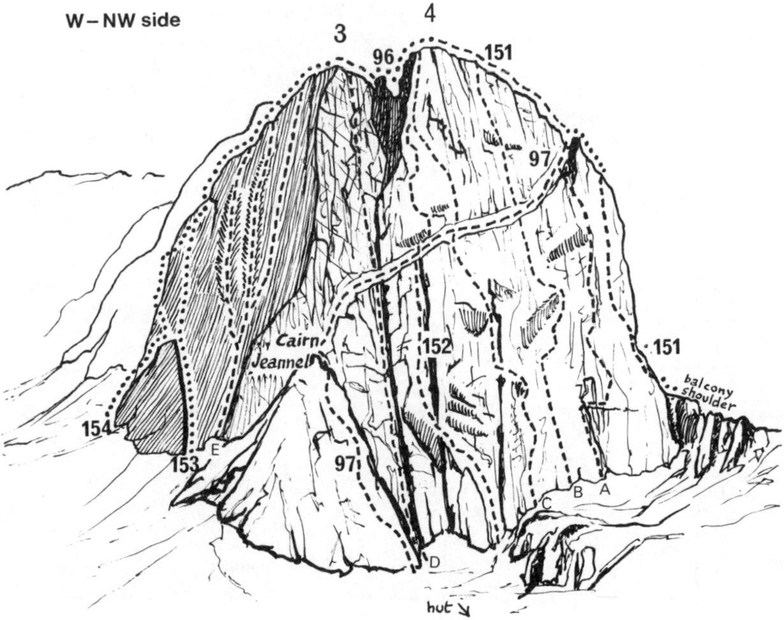

A Dièdres route (V+) B Overhangs route (V+) C Direct route (IV)

D Central Couloir (V–) E Peak 3, NW face routes. Left, Thérond (V); centre, Direct (V+); right, Vernet (IV)

GRAND GENDARME OF THE CAYRE DE L'AGNEL 2789m.

Prominent tower forming S buttress of the Cayre de l'Agnel (R.99,100),
R of the Col de la Ruine (R.101). Short but worthwhile routes. Reached
from Cougourde hut in $1\frac{1}{2}$–$1\frac{3}{4}$h. Some maps give height as 2779m.

155. South Face. Quite fine, 100m., V. Mme.C.Kogan, Mlle. F.
Cravoisier, M.Dufranc, C.Ferretti, E.Isch-Wall, 15 June,1958.
A chimney leads to top of a pillar, then take a slab on L to a Y shaped
crack. Ascend this (IV,IV+) and exit by the L branch (V, peg). Then
the ridge to top ($1\frac{1}{2}$ h).

156. South-West Ridge. Excellent and sustained, 100m.,V. Michel
& Mme.Dufranc, R.Prangé, 4 September,1956. Start R of ridge then
gain and follow crest (IV,IV+ & V-). Where it steepens move R and
rejoin the crest; follow it to top (V & IV+) ($1\frac{1}{2}$ h.).

157. West Face. Quite good and continuous, 100m., V. A.Blond-
eau, L.Castelli, J.Ciffréo, 28 June,1953. A couloir is found round
the L side of SW ridge. L of this climb a groove (IV-) to enter and
follow couloir (III) where an overhang is avoided L (IV & V,peg). So
continue up couloir to top ($1\frac{1}{4}$ h.).

158. North Ridge. The longest climb on the gendarme, interesting
and fairly sustained, 200m., V. F.Cravoisier, M.Dufranc, 8 July,
1961. Approach as for R.98,101 to reach foot of the snowy, often
icy N couloir dividing gendarme R from parent mtn. ($1\frac{3}{4}$ h.). Cross
snow R at bottom of couloir and climb a chimney with loose blocks R
of ridge crest to a shoulder. Climb a crack (V) then join a crack
continuing the chimney line (IV & V,pegs). Cross to L of ridge and
ascend a double crack section on L again (IV & V, peg). Now take
a couloir to top ($3\frac{1}{2}$ h.).

Descent, via the Gap. Go down steep steps NE to gap (III) and so
descend the S/SE couloir, scree and grass (45 min.).

CAYRE DES ERPS 2501m.

Situated above the lower Guilié cwm (Erps valley), approached from
Le Boréon by R.19 in $1\frac{3}{4}$ h. This fine tower terminates the WNW ridge
of the Cayres Nègres (Pelago spur), from which it is separated by a
significant gap. It offers numerous top quality climbs on excellent,
rough rock.

CAYRE DES ERPS NW-W-SW sides

159. <u>North-West Buttress and North Face</u>. A combination of routes made in 1952/53, resulting in a very direct climb of good quality. Tiny stances, 200m., V-.

At L side of tower, start R of the foot of NW buttress, below a dièdre closed by overhangs. Ascend a wall towards the first overhang; now traverse to turn it L and belay on small pillar (30m., V-, IV, peg). Go up a short wall/slab and return R to dièdre. Climb to an overhang; traverse R and take a wall to foot of a crack (30m., V-, V, then III, peg). Climb crack and exit L (30m., V-, peg). A wall leads to a terrace (20m., III+). Continue by an obvious crack, then move R and using a small crack reach a large grass terrace (30m., III+ then IV). Follow the terrace L for 30m. and climb a gully by crack on its L side (25m., III+). Cross a detached flake, climb a short dièdre and exit L (15m., IV, peg) to finish up 60m. of pleasant slabs (II) (2½ h.).

160. <u>West Buttress</u>. A fine sustained climb, 200m., V+ & A2, 30-35 pegs. G. Barrata, F. Ruggeri, B. Salesi, D. Ughetto, 20 September, 1964.

Start some 15m. L of the Great West Crack and 10m. R of NW buttress, just L of a parallel line of subsidiary cracks. Climb a shallow groove for a few m. then gain a little pillar on L. Climb R on to ledges (IV & V, pegs), an overhanging flake, then a dièdre and traverse L to a terrace (30m., A1 & V, pegs). Mount a very steep wall (12m.) and traverse L past a short overhanging wall to gain a slab, followed by moving up to R (IV, V & V+, A1, pegs). This leads to a niche in a grassy gully forming the upper part of the subsidiary cracks. Ascend with flaky holds on its R (IV & V+, pegs). Take an overhanging wall and a slab above, lichen (A1 & V+, pegs). Now several m. on N side to an overhanging dièdre. Jam up 8m. (VI/A2), then another 8m. (A2) and surmount the upper overhang (A1/V+, pegs); terrace. In 6m. another terrace and a 4m. wall (IV). Traverse a ledge R to crest below the final step. Climb a crack (8m), turn overhang by moving 2m. L and return R by a slab to good terrace (20m., V, IV, pegs). A short movement L, then easy rocks to top (6 h.).

161. <u>Great West Crack</u>. The big crack slanting up W face, forming a gully in lower part and a chimney higher up. It finishes at a little gap with a bridged block. 225m., V+, A2. G. Chabert, G. Demenge, 19 October, 1954.

Directly below crack, start up a vague grassy chimney (15m., IV+, peg). Then avoid overhanging rock by a slab R (V+) and climb 10m. to scree (V). Enter and climb bed to surmount an overhang (V); continue for 20m. to below a slight bulge (V, IV). Here exit up a wall R (V+, pegs) and go up for 10m. to rejoin chimney at a poor stance (V, pegs). Climb

20m. to a niche in a large chockstone (IV). Traverse 5m. to top of the block (V). Climb 12m. by layback (IV+), then up an overhang to gap in NW ridge (V+). Continue for a few m. to a terrace where the W buttress route is joined and followed to top (6 h.).

West Face (Voie des Barbus). A very fine, sustained climb, 200m., V+ & A2. Starts 20m.R of Great West Crack; takes wall direct, avoiding a major L-hand variation at the pegged lower yellow roof.

162. South-West Pillar. A magnificent climb, probably the best, but not the hardest, on the tower. 220m., V, A1, 15 pegs. J.Chabrier, F.Cravoisier, M.Dufranc, 24 & 31 August, 1958.

Not far from the S couloir, start a few m. L of a big dièdre bounding pillar on R. Climb the wall of a yellow depression from L to R till below an overhang. Surmount this, move L, ascend 4m., then move L again to a stance (25m., A1,V,IV+,pegs). Return R then steep slabs and a dièdre, finishing R on a small pillar. Reach a sloping break at foot of a wall; ascend latter to a platform (25m., IV+,IV, peg). Take wall on R then a chimney line to large grass ledge. Follow ledge L to highest point, at foot of vague dièdre closed by an overhang (25m., IV,III then 10m. easy). Climb R then steep bit to overhang; move R and up to small stance (20m.,IV+,V, pegs). Move R again and get on to a vague pillar. Exit L (hard), go up a wall and traverse R to stance on a platform near the S Chimney (20m.,V,IV+). Return L, go up a short overhanging crack then a steep wall. Move R and climb an overhanging wall to continue direct to grass terrace (30m., V,IV,IV+,pegs). From terrace reach top of a little pillar, at foot of a Y crack (10m., III). Climb crack on L by a slab, then by bed and exit R (25m., V,V+, pegs/wedge). Descend one m. L, pull up to and climb a large flake crack. Traverse L and take a crack system to terrace (30m., IV). Now go direct (III) to top ($4\frac{1}{2}$ h.).

South Chimney. The chimney cutting the S facet to a grassy terrace near summit gives a fine sustained route. 180m., V+. Starts just below rock bridge in the S couloir which comes down from the Cayre gap.

Descent. Leave summit along E rib, first on L side then R, to descend a step by a dièdre (III) into Cayre gap. On the flank of the parent mtn. follow a ledge system L(N), cross a gully and go up its L side for 30m. to resume the ledge system running N round a buttress, crossing a smooth slab (5m., III). Continue traverse with narrower ledges on to a 2nd buttress and cross a vague saddle to the far side and easy slabs leading N into a big scree gully. Descend this to bottom and scree slope N of the tower base. 45 min. down, $1\frac{1}{4}$ h.up.

The gullies either side (N & S) of the Cayre gap are III+/IV+ respectively, quite awkward in descent, and some danger from loose rock. The S one is used not infrequently by climbers, with abseils.

TETE DES TABLASSES

See R.110,111. The N (Ital.) side of this mtn. has a number of important rock climbs, notably the NW ridge of S top (500m., V) and the N buttress of the SW ridge (200m., V, then 200m. easy).

POINTE GIEGN

See R.115. As noted previously many routes have been made along the complicated SW wall of this mtn., some rated among the best of their class in the Mercantour Park. The approach from the Col de Salèse by way of going round the Colombrons shoulder is tedious but little more than 2 h.

The NW ridge of the mtn. turns N at pt. 2825m. to reach the Margiole (2852m.). At this pt. a long subsidiary ridge descends SW, thus dividing the SW cliffs of the mtn. into a small area facing W (to the N of this dividing ridge) and the main SW cliffs themselves running under the NW ridge to the summit line, and beyond where a short stretch faces W under the S ridge. All the climbs are on prominent buttresses, pillars and couloir/dièdres in this SW/W facing barrier of cliffs. The notable features, marked by the ridge profile, are from L (N) to R (S):

Jumeaux du Giegn (2800m.) (W face, 250m., V); Pt. 2825m. (Punta Maria André) where the subsidiary dividing ridge originates - lower down this ridge the NW buttress of pt. 2622m. gives a dièdre of 160m., V+; Brèche du Giegn (2795m.), the lowest pt. on main ridge between Pt. Giegn and the Margiole; Last Gendarme (S pillar, 200m., IV+); NW Gendarme (SW face, 250m., V); Grand Gendarme (SW face rtes, 300m., V/V+; SW dièdre, 300m., IV+); NW summit, Tour des Choucas, perhaps the most famous climb hereabouts, two main lines (300m., V+); Pt. Giegn (SW face, 300m., IV+); S shoulder (W buttress, 250m., V-).

CAYRE DU PREFOUNS

See main heading and introductions to R.113,114. The mtn. is a remarkable ridge of granite pinnacles, smooth and steep. The lower part of the frontier ridge, immediately above the Pas du Préfouns, is called the Aigs. du Lac Nègre.

163. **Main Ridge Traverse**. A long, varied and interesting expedition with soft options. IV-, not sustained. D.-L.Bianco, M.Campia, G. Ellena, 19 September,1948.

From the Pas du Préfouns (R.112) go up a grassy slope and rocks to 1st gendarme of the Aigs.du Lac Nègre and descend to gap beyond. In the gap traverse 3m. L and climb a couloir/chimney (20m.,III+), followed by easier rocks to top of 2nd gendarme. Down easy rocks R and up the 3rd gendarme by its crest. Down the SW side to Brèche E des Jumeaux (II+). A 10m. chimney/crack, undercut at the bottom, starts the ascent of Jumeaux E, then a short wall and a mantelshelf R to a detached flake. An exposed stride back on to the face allows a wall to be climbed to top (IV-, stride IV+). Descend the SW side to the Brèche des Jumeaux. Now ascend 4m. R and traverse 3m. L to an obvious crack. Take this to stepped ledges and the top of Jumeaux W (IV, peg). Now abseil into Brèche W des Jumeaux. (All this section can be avoided by R.114).

From Brèche W take crest (III) of the 6th gendarme and descend to the Brèche des Aigs. du Lac Nègre (similarly avoidable by R.114). Now follow crest to the E Peak of Préfouns (III, with a short crack and one move of IV). Descend SW side to E gap of Préfouns (E peak can be avoided on S side). Climb the Central peak, either on the R (N)side (II) or by a buttress on the L (S) (III) ($3\frac{1}{2}$ h. from the Pas). Continue traverse to descend by R.113.

South Face. Approached as for R.113. A number of tapering buttresses rise into the pinnacled summit ridge of the Préfouns proper. A terrace cuts them about one third way up, and long gullies divide the salient masses. Several routes have been made here, about 250m., from III to V+. Good rock but sometimes discontinuous climbing.

East Face (of N ridge). Situated in Italy, the least visited (from France) but the most impressive face of the mtn., forming a prelude to the Cresta Savoia which develops further R (N). Easily reached from the Pas (R.112) in 15 min. Approach from Questa hut, 45 min. Furthest R is the most famous climb on this face, the E Pillar of the rockhead standing above the Sella di Préfouns (2715m.), the gap dividing the end of the Préfouns N ridge from the continuation as the Cresta Savoia; 300m.,V+,A1, with a pitch of IV to continue along main N ridge. Further L the lower wall of the face gives two sustained climbs of 300m.,V, then the E face couloir (IV). L again, almost in the summit line, a dièdre system gives another route of IV+/V.

CRESTA SAVOIA   E side   R.164

Punta Ultimo N di Préfouns (E Pillar)
Sella di Préfouns
Maria
Giovanna
Mafalda
Umberto
Iolanda
Antecima
Questa hut
Pas du Préfouns
Préfouns N ridge
Préfouns E face
Préfouns cwm

CRESTA SAVOIA

Jutting into Italy the N ridge of the Cayre du Préfouns drops to a gap, Sella di Préfouns (2715m.). It then continues in a remarkable series of ridge towers of chamonix-type granite, the Cresta Savoia. From the gap these are: P.Maria (2790m.), P.Giovanna (2780m.), P.Mafalda (2750m.), P.Umberto (2740m.), P.Iolanda (2670m.) and the Antecima (c.2600m.). These pts. are separated by significant gaps and the ridge up to the Cayre from the Sella gap is of similar character. The Cresta Savoia is the only important mtn. feature in the Maritime Alps for which no reference in English mountaineering literature can be found.

164. <u>Traverse North-South</u>. A magnificent climb on excellent rough rock. About 600m. of climbing, IV on the whole, pitches of III,IV & V. A.Frisoni, G.Zapparoli-Manzoni, 17-18 September,1924. From the Questa hut on W side a track and rough slopes lead up to the Antecima ($\frac{3}{4}$ h.), then abseil to gap below. Or cross the Préfouns col (R.112) and descend main track on Ital. side to E base of the Antecima, where slanting grass rakes lead up towards its summit, but traverse up L as soon as possible to enter the Antecima-Iolanda gap (II).

From this gap climb N shoulder of Iolanda rather R of crest, then take crest to top. Abseil 25m. into next gap. Climb a crack with an overhanging exit (V, crux of route), then crest to top of Umberto (III). Down to next gap. Climb slabs L of crest, then by crest to an open groove on R (IV), and so to top of Mafalda. Down to next gap, and ascend L of crest, then on crest to Giovanna. Down to next gap, climb R of crest, regain it by a dièdre (IV) and follow up to Maria (3 h.). Descend to the Sella gap either by crest or R flank. Above it climb a wall to reach the crest (III+). Continue to a gendarme which is climbed rather R of the crest, finishing up a groove (IV); or avoid it R. Follow the very narrow ridge to a false summit, then on to the N peak of the Cayre ($2\frac{1}{2}$ h., $5\frac{1}{4}$ h. from foot of Antecima).

Most parties will descend the W gully of the Sella di Préfouns, easy rubble, into the Portettes cwm above (S of) the Questa hut. The easiest way back into France is over Brèche Margiole (2739m.), steep scree and blocks.

<u>East and West Faces</u>. The 5 towers of the Cresta Savoia are covered with routes. The best ones predominate on the E side, and originate mostly from Ital. climbers in the 1950s and 60s. Summary: Maria, E face, 2 rtes., 250m., V & V+. Giovanna, ESE ridge, 250m.,V+,also face rtes. Mafalda, SE ridge, 250m.,IV, also face rtes; W face,120m, IV+. Umberto, SE ridge, 300m.,IV+; E face, 300m.,IV+/V; W face, 120m.,IV+. Iolanda, E face, 250m.,IV-.

CIMA DI NASTA   W side

summit
NW
SW
SW ridge
SW gendarme
166
165
Colle di Nasta
Paganini
W Couloir (see Cima Paganini in text)

NASTA

Warning about snow/ice conditions given in main introduction, R.116.

165. West Buttress (Spigolo de la Nasta). A famous, popular and very classic climb on excellent red rock, with a fine mountaineering air. The buttress rises to the NW summit. 325m., overall IV-. G.Bonjean, J.Vernet, 19 June,1932.

From the Remondino hut ascend directly to foot of buttress, where till late in season steep snow is usually found (45 min.). Start at lowest pt. and climb to a steep band, turned by a chimney slanting R (50m., and 50m.,III+). Go up a couloir beside buttress for 2 pitches (40m.,easy) then join crest at an obvious saddle above a vertical section. Take the exposed buttress by a series of walls, cracks and chimneys to a shoulder below summit (6 pitches of 25m.,IV-, sustained, one bit of IV+). From shoulder climb a wall slightly R of an obvious crack; after 8m. traverse L into crack, which is followed to top (40m.,IV). Crack direct from bottom, harder (3 h.).

166. West Buttress of SW Summit. This flat-faced buttress runs parallel with the previous one, across a big couloir to R. A good route for moderate performers, 300m.,III. B.&F.Salesi, 3 August,1958.

Approach as for the Spigolo. Start further R, at foot of buttress, and between the entrances to gullies L and R (45 min.). An initial crest of 90m. leads to a shoulder. Trend L, across the base of a gully, and go up a pillar to the wall above. In this take a crack R for 5m.(III) then trend L up short steps to a long crack. Climb this (III) to a position L of a gendarme. Climb direct to crest above (IV) and continue on crest over blocks to a shoulder (III). Traverse briefly R under steep rock to climb a cracked slab (III), then trend L to the final steepness. Climb this, avoiding a red step L, and continue directly to top (3 h.).

SW Ridge, over the S/SW Gendarme and SW summit, fine mountaineering route, II/III with a pitch of IV.

West Face, the wall L of the Spigolo, 300m., III/IV.

MADRE DI DIO

167. East-West Traverse. For topography, see main entry. A long route similar to the Cresta Savoia, and about the same standard with pitches of III,IV & V. Reach the Colletto Freshfield by R.120. Climb E ridge of the Cima dei Camosci, first by a ramp on L, then a

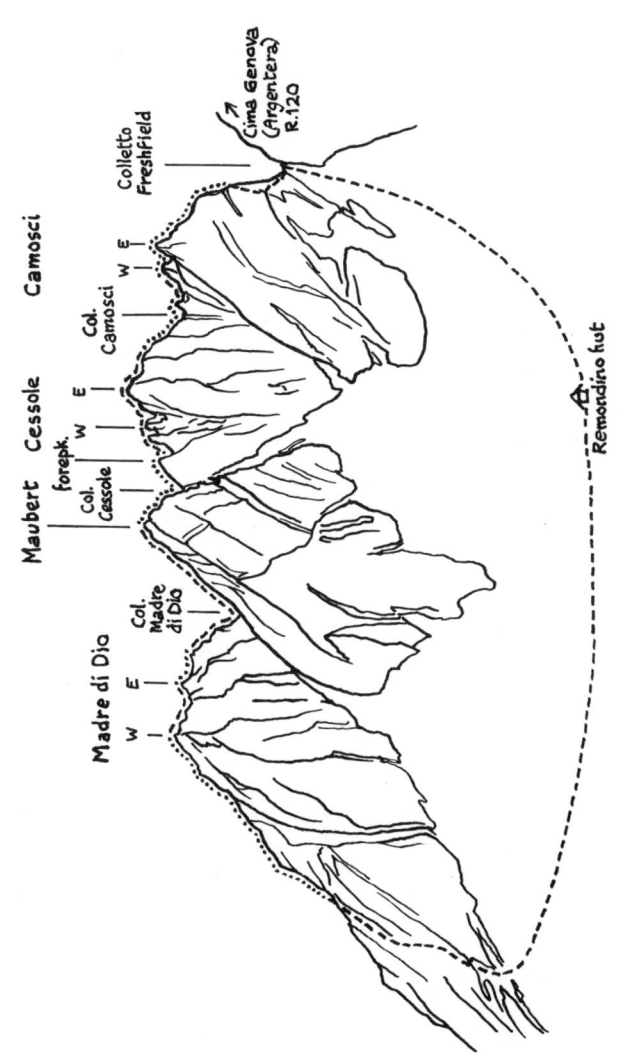

slab R. Cross the ridge to a chimney on NE side then go up to top (30 min.). Down to next gap and turn the E ridge of W peak by a ledge on N side to join the W ridge. Follow it to W top and descend to the Colletto dei Camosci. Ascend the E ridge of Cima di Cessole by a buttress on the L (IV), then by the ridge (III+). Climb down and make a short abseil to a terrace on N side between the twin tops. Go up a steep wall L (IV, peg) to rejoin the ridge. Move R and back to reach the W peak (IV). Descend exposed ridge N to a gap and climb a forepeak. The ridge and 2 abseils of 40m. & 20m. gain the Colletto di Cessole (3 h.). A buttress on the E ridge of Cima Maubert leads to a gap; the subsequent wall (III+) and a crack (III) allows the ridge above to be attained and followed to top. Down the W ridge, first L then direct. Traverse L to an oblique ledge descending R to the Colletto della Madre di Dio (2720m.) (1½ h.). Climb 15m. on poor rock up the E ridge of the Madre di Dio, then a gully full of loose blocks to an exposed terrace. A short cracked wall on R (V-, peg) is followed to a gap below a yellow tower (III). Traverse L (S) on a ledge. Continue for 25m. (III+, delicate) and rejoin ridge which is followed to the E peak (1 h.). On to the W peak where grassy ledges and gullies lead down the W face (45 min., 7 h. from Freshfield col).

ARGENTERA

West Face Buttresses. Apart from R.122, this face between the skyline pts. of the Forcella couloir (L) and La Spalla (R) is marked by parallel buttresses giving some of the longest expeditions in the district. The biggest of these, the Promontoire, offers serious mixed climbing, 1050m, III+/IV, variable starts and other variations higher up. The buttress directly below the S Peak is a simpler line but steeper and more difficult, 800m., IV+. About 100m. R is a similar buttress of IV. Under La Spalla is another L slanting buttress of 700m., III, with liberal amounts of snow/ice in parts. The Spalla wall, R.121, is to the R again. All these routes are conveniently approached in 30-45 min. from Bozano hut.

Gelas di Lourousa. There are 2 good rock climbs on the great slab L of the Canalone Günther (R.122, footnote), starting just above the foot of latter. One goes up the centre of this SW facet (fine rock, III-), the other up the L edge on a ridge (III/IV+), about 600m.

CORNO STELLA
S side

CORNO STELLA 3050m.

The mtn. most coveted by climbers in the Maritime Alps, with an international reputation. The easiest routes are IV. A superb rock peak of curious form – the name alludes to a 'pointed hoof'. The steeply inclined summit ridge roof is highest at the SE end. The walls either side vary from 300 to 600m. high. Rock generally very good. As a spur of the Gelas di Lourousa (Argentera) it encloses the N side of the Argentera W cwm in which the Bozano hut is found.

South Side. All routes here are easily reached by a myriad of tracks from the Bozano hut in 45 min. or less. The climbs below are taken from L to R.

168. Diagonal Route. A magnificent climb, probably the best on the S cliff, taking a brownish diagonal line weaving its way between overhangs. 500m., V+, very sustained. Rock difficult to peg. Finish by Campia Route. M. & Mme. Dufranc, 15 August, 1968.

Start round corner L of lowest pt. of face. Just L of the diagonal break climb a parallel crack (IV+), then cross a slab L (V, V+, peg) to reach a ledge below the diagonal. Traverse a grey slab L (V+, peg) then climb a dièdre on its L (IV). Back on to the slab and traverse R and down onto the diagonal (IV+, peg). Climb it for several m. then take a parallel weakness through a grey slab to the R (V, peg). Gain a little shoulder on L. Follow the diagonal (V, peg) and climb a smooth wall near the lower band of overhangs (V+, blade peg). A smooth groove (V & V+, peg) leads to a gully and a shoulder at the highest pt. of the big grass band crossing the S face. Finish up next route (7 h.).

169. Campia Route. Fine climbing but uneven standard and difficult pegging. Water washed in top part when summit snow is melting. 500m., III to the grass band, V to the quartz vein, and III above that. M. Campia, G. Ellena, R. Nervo, 15 July, 1945.

Start at lowest pt. of face and go up a gully/chimney, then grassy slabs on R to the high pt. of the grass band (1½ h.). Climb a buttress directly above on loose holds (IV), then 2 dièdres obliquely L. When the face steepens take a short steep wall (V, peg) then a slab to a terrace (IV+, delicate). The wall above is limited high up on L by a dièdre. Traverse L then zigzag up a slab, finishing by a delicate stride L into the dièdre. Now climb this (IV+ & V). Traverse 5m. R on a slippery ledge with poor holds, then a good ledge (V then IV, peg). Now a steep black wall on good holds (III+). Take an overhang on L (V, peg) then a chimney and exit R to the quartz band (IV). Take it for a few m., then climb a ramp slanting up L to summit plateau ($4\frac{1}{2}$ h, 6 h. for climb).

170. <u>Kosterlitz Variation</u>. From the grass band this offers a more difficult and quite independent finish for the Diagonal and Campia routes. V+, sustained, 15 pegs. G.C.Grassi, M.Kosterlitz, 3 October, 1970.

At the grass band climb the Campia buttress with loose holds (III) for 35m., then move R to below an overhang closing the wall 40m. higher. Climb a slab/wall R (III/III+) to an easy ledge line. Descend R and by a ramp reach some blocks. Climb 2m. then traverse a wall R (IV) to go round its R edge and along to below a vertical wall; move R under this to stance. Climb a chimney/groove for 12m.(V), then ridge to R and cracked slabs (IV) to foot of a yellow slanting dièdre at the quartz band. Climb bed to a leaning flake and traverse R. Continue dièdre to surmount an overhang R. Resume climbing dièdre bed to below a big flake roof (V+). Turn this on L (35m., V/V+). Go up back of the dièdre for 4m. and exit R in moving round a slightly overhanging rib (V). Then direct climbing to a good stance/terrace (IV-). Trending L, continue by a ramp and slabs (IV), then directly to top (4 h.).

<u>Central Route</u>. Runs up middle of S face, VI,A1 or V+,A2. Several artificial pitches, generally pegged up.

171. <u>Cessole Route</u>. The most frequented and famous climb on the mtn. but not the easiest. Varied and interesting, 400m., IV, not sustained. Key pitches often wet. First ascensionists.

Start at R end of face directly below summit. Climb easy rocks to the grass band; follow this up L edge of a short grassy gully to first grass terrace of this rake system. From upper L end of terrace, climb in a gully/crack of black rock coming down from a black roof, for about 20m. (III+). Then go up wall to its L, followed by a delicate traverse R (IV) to rejoin a crack and the groove just below the black roof. Traverse R again across and up slabs for 60m. (III) to the quartz band, which crosses the face. The quartz is interrupted by steep rock cut by 2 chimneys. Take the R-hand one to a stance. Ignore an easy grass traverse R. Climb trending L into an open hollow and up a chimney/gully to reach a break below an overhanging black crag. Climb the shiny slab L of it, the Mauvais Pas (22m., IV & IV+, peg), platform. Climb a crack slanting L (10m.) and exit L over a little overhang (IV-, peg). Continue slanting L on slabs (25m.,III), traverse R, surmount a short overhang (III+) then take a hanging grassy gully, and via a gap and final wall (30m.,III) emerge on summit ridge (4 h.).

<u>South Face Direct</u>. Starts 100m. up couloir below the F. del Gelas di Lourousa, directly under and to R of summit line. Steep compact rock difficult to peg, small stances, 450m., V+/VI/A2. Several variations, minor and major. The best partly artificial route on the face (1960)(9 h.).

172. <u>North-West Ridge</u>. The S face is crossed by all the grass band to reach the start proper. The easiest route to the summit, invariably used for descent. 300m. from the Forcella gap, III sustained, with bits of IV. G.Ellena, L.Giuliano, 21 August, 1927.

Follow the Cessole route to L upper end of 1st grass terrace. Continue up the R side of a little gully, then in the bed to a small gap, from where a 2nd terrace is reached. This is a rock covered slope; cross it horizontally to just below Forcella at far end. Above is a grassy gully rising to top of 1st step in NW ridge. Go L, beyond this gully, and climb a vertical twisting crack (III+) to the Forcella (1 h.). From gap climb crest for 15m. (III+) to a small terrace. Traverse R, descending slightly along a ledge line to reach a break in gully bed which drops down to the grass band. Climb bed, up a slightly overhanging wall (IV) and into a chimney (III+/III) leading to crest at top of first ridge step. Now by doubtful rock on the L (N) side to top of next step and up a big slab to final step. The R edge of a dièdre with good holds (III) leads to an overhang and an exit R (III+) to a little terrace on the R (S). A short strenuous groove leads to an exposed slab under a big overhang. Follow a little ledge obliquely R nearly to the overhang (IV-), then another obliquely L back to ridge (IV, exposed). Continue to a little terrace, then a short gully leads to NW end of summit roof (4-5 h.).
Note: It is possible to climb a crack L of the gully rising from grass band (and R of one used to reach the Forcella), so avoiding excursion via the Forcella gap (III+).

<u>Descent</u>. From the NW top, turn a short step on L and go down slightly R to the head of a narrow couloir on N side. From a fixed peg abseil 20m. to a platform somewhat to the L. From another belay, abseil 20m. down the L side to a small terrace. From another belay abseil 20m. down a dièdre to a large slab. Climb down the step below on the R and regain the crest at the top of the S couloir, at top of 1st step. Now make 3 abseils of 25m., 20m., 20m. down the couloir to the grass band. Do not attempt to climb or descend the couloir directly below the Forcella, IV+, awkward.

<u>North Flank</u>. This forbidding wall, 600m. high, flanks the Lourousa couloir (R.123) and is perhaps the most serious rock climbing venue in the Maritime Alps. There are three main route lines, all quite direct, rising to the SE and NW summits, and the other up the centre of the

wall. That to the SE summit is rated VI,A3. F.Ruggeri, D.Ughetto, 11-13 June,1962. The Varrone biv. hut is the best starting point.

GUIDES' CHAIN

This jagged ridge extends W from the Corno Stella. The main summits are named after early guides of the region and are, from E to W: P. Ghigo (2898m.), P. Piacenza (2772m.), P. Plent (2747m.).

<u>Complete Traverse, West-East</u>. A first rate expedition of reasonable standard, varied, mainly III with pitches of IV. The descent is normally made by the grass band crossing the S face of the Corno Stella, as used by R.172, but an enterprising party will continue up the NW ridge of the Stella by latter route. R.Chabod, G.Derege, M.Rivero, 25 August,1927.

173. From the Bozano hut work up below the Chain to foot of P.2710 and climb a couloir slanting steeply L to grassy rocks, which are followed R to the top of P.2710 ($1\frac{1}{2}$ h.). Follow the stepped ridge, turn a gendarme on the L, climb a step direct (III) and follow the sharp horizontal crest to the Forcella Plent (1 h.). Above, turn a gendarme on the L and reach a gap with a knife edge block. Climb a wall above (IV) to a break on R of the crest. A vertical crack (IV) on R leads to a stance on crest. Turn a short riser on L and climb a red dièdre R of the crest. The ridge eases and leads to P. Plent (1 h.). Descend a wall by a dièdre (III), the crest then the L side to the Forcella della P. Bifida (30 min.). Traverse the crest of the twin tops of P. Bifida (II) to the Forcella Piacenza (30 min.). Follow the steep crest (III), easing to the horizontal, up to P. Piacenza (30 min.). Continue till an abseil gains the Forcella del Ciat (15 min.). Traverse over the next two gendarmes (III-) to the Forcella del Lup (30 min.). A grey wall leads up the next gendarme (or turn L) and a crack goes down to top of a yellow step. Descend this (III). A 40m. horizontal knife edge, a descent to a gap, then the crest, or a slab on R, leads up to Pta. Ghigo ($1\frac{1}{2}$ h.).
Descend broken rocks in a narrow couloir, traverse a sharp gendarme then abseil down a thin yellow-red edge to the W gap of the Forcella del Corno. Turn the Piccolo Corno in the gap on the L and reach the E gap, at the foot of the NW ridge of the Corno Stella (45 min.). From here use R.172 to regain hut, or continue to top of latter peak.
Most of the difficulties can be avoided by descents and re-ascents,and the round trip, hut to hut without Corno Stella, will take about 9 h.

<u>South Face</u>. Many good routes on the individual peaks of the Guides' Chain are easily approached from the Bozano hut.

GUIDES' CHAIN   S side

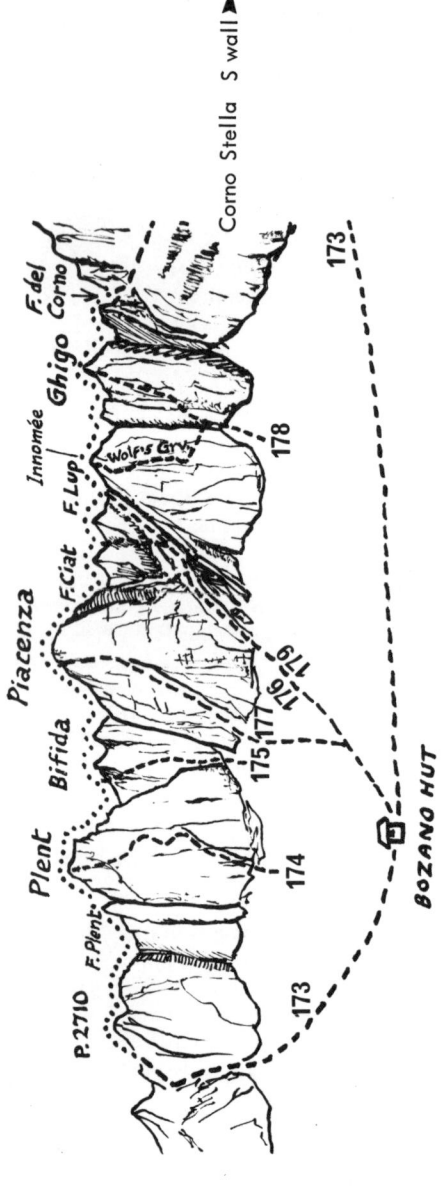

Punta Plent

The square top immediately E of Forcella Plent.

174. South Face. A nice climb, reasonably continuous, 200m., IV.
G.Ellena, E.Soria, 28 June, 1931.

Gain the foot of a couloir on the R and climb its slippery lower tier by a short but strenuous struggle. Climb the couloir obliquely to a ledge on the SE ridge (IV,peg). Traverse slightly L, turn a buttress and go up a chimney to a platform. Climb a white slab on poor holds (IV, pegs) and cross an inclined slab L to a saddle in centre of the face, below the summit. Climb 40m. of easy angled but exposed slabs to an overhanging red wall. Go L, first by an exposed ledge, then a delicate wall to a little gendarme near the SW ridge. Exposed slabs on R lead to a couloir of loose red rock and the top (3-4 h.).
Descend the W ridge and abseil 35m. to a gap; then turn a tower on R (N) side to reach the Forcella Plent. Descend the S couloir near the ridge forming its R (W) side. At the bottom traverse L (E) over steep ground to rejoin the scree ($1\frac{1}{2}$ h.).

Punta Bifida

175. South Buttress. A good sustained climb, 200m., IV+. B. & F. Salesi, 3 June, 1962. Start up a big dièdre in the buttress bounding the couloir falling from the gap between Bifida and Plent on the R. After 20m. it bends R (IV,IV+). Take a white gully/groove on R (IV), past a good stance on a flake, then traverse horizontally L for 10m. to a buttress (IV). Climb it (IV,IV+, peg). Then a gully/ledge slanting R and some slabs above it (IV,IV+, peg) leading to another gully/ledge. Go up R for 15m. (III) and come out L of the top (III) (3 h.).
Descend by the W ridge to gap below P. Plent. Go 40m. down its N couloir and traverse under Plent. Ascend to the Forcella Plent and descend as for R.174.

Punta Piacenza

176. The easiest route up and down the peak from the Bozano hut is that to the Forcella del Lup (q.v. below), to the final easy couloir leading to the ridge gap. Cross this couloir and climb up L to the gap between the two Ciat/Lup gendarmes on the main ridge. Turn the W gendarme on R and descend to Forcella del Ciat, below the steep ridge (IV) of the peak. From this col descend a few m. R (N), traverse L on a ledge and climb a short couloir to the summit ($1\frac{1}{2}$ h. from hut, II/II+, short pitch of III).

177. South Face. A classic route on excellent rock, following a prominent chimney. 200m., IV+. D.-L.Bianco, G.Ellena, E.Soria, 14 September, 1930.

Start at L side of face and make a rising traverse L over slabs to foot of a wide chimney, closed higher up by an overhang. After a few m. in the chimney (blocked) get on to rounded rib on the R (IV+). A smooth slab follows (IV) and the chimney can be rejoined. Continue to a dièdre, reached by a delicate traverse on small holds (IV). Climb the smooth dièdre and slab above it. Move R on to buttress, climbed by an exposed pitch (IV) and return to chimney. Easier climbing for 50m. then turn an overhang R. At another blockage climb a short wall (IV), then grassy rocks to below a red overhang. Turn this R by a slab on friable holds. Traverse L to a grassy ledge and rejoin chimney, now a gully. Ascend this then ridge on R; exit direct to a narrow ledge on R. Cross ledge and climb a wall direct (IV), then traverse L to rejoin couloir. Ascend this, easing to summit ($3\frac{1}{2}$ h.).
Descend by the narrow E ridge and with an abseil, etc. gain the Forcella Ciat. Turn the 1st gendarme on N side, and from gap beyond descend S, turning L to a grassy slope. So join the Forcella Lup descent.

Punta Innomée, Wolf's Groove. Starts from chimney slanting L of Punta Ghigo and after a pitch exits L to reach and follow a groove/chimney system. A splendid and very sustained climb, one of the best routes in the area. 200m., V,A2, 60 pegs. J.Baratta, F.Ruggeri, B.Salesi, D. Ughetto, 8 & 10 May, 8 October, 1965.

Punta Ghigo

178. South-West Face. An interesting climb, 200m., IV. G.Ellena, E.Soria, 14 July, 1929. Start at foot of slanting chimney/gully at the L side of face. Climb it to where it narrows and break out R to a big scree terrace. Climb a steep slab and slant up R to a platform (25m., IV, delicate). A steep black wall (30m., III) brings an easing of the angle where the route bears up R to a horizontal ledge. 30m. straight up to summit ridge, followed N to top (3-4 h.).
Descend SE ridge and abseil to a detached pink flake. From here go to the col between Ghigo and P.Corno and turn its gendarme on the N side (exposed) to gain the Forcella del Corno. Return by R.172 ($2\frac{1}{2}$ h.).

Forcella del Lup   2750m.

179. Between the 2nd and 3rd gendarmes on main ridge, as found between the F. del Ciat (L) and summit of Ghigo (R). The easiest way on

to and off the main ridge. Lup=Ghigo's nickname. Ciat=Piacenza's (the cat). II+ with a move of III. At foot of P. Piacenza S wall, at R side two parallel grooves rise R. Take L one and work up progressively to R, to a break in the rib separating the 2 grooves. Climb rib for 20m. to a gendarme, traverse a little down to R (slab,III) and so reach an obvious scree terrace. On the R climb a crack (3m.) then the R-hand couloir groove to a narrow grassy gully leading to a grass terrace. Ascend L, then up a chimney (5m.) leading to a ridge bordering L side of couloir. Cross ridge and climb couloir to col (1 h.).

The Lup N side couloir is liable to stonefall. Rather more than halfway down, after a branch coming in from the Ciat col, a wide ledge line can be followed R, facing out, which gives access to the base of the Lourousa couloir. This is the shortest access from the Bozano hut to this couloir and the N face of the Corno Stella.

Index

Adus hut 32
Agnel, Cayre de l' 79
- Cime de l' 78
- Gd. Gend. de l' 79,125
André, Brèche 72
- Pointe 72,119
Argentera, Cima 98,136
Arpette, Pas de l' 43,44
Asta peaks 33
Authion, L' 42
Autier, Baisse du Lac 46,47
- Cayre 47
- Tête du Lac 47
Azur 2000 12,13

Baissette, Baisse de 35,82
- Cime de 35,83
Barbero biv. hut 33
Barel, Cayres 115
Barn, Col du 108
Bastione, Il 95
Basto, Baisse de 26,27,47
- Têtes du 47
Baus biv. hut 33
- Cima del 95
Bego, Mont 37,38,43
Belvédère 19,23
Bessons, Collet des Lacs 81
- Tête des Lacs 35
Bianco hut, D.-L. 106
Bifida, Pta. 143
Bollène, La 42
Boréon, Le 19,23
- valley 30
Bozano hut 36
Bresses, Tête N des 86
- Tête S des 86
Brocan, Cima del 95

Cabrera, Pso. 106
Cabret, Cime 64
Camosci, Cima dei 96

Capelet, Gd. 45
Castérine valley 37
Caval, Mt. 73
Cavaline, Baisse 42
Cayre, Baisse du Pt. 69
- Brèche du 69
- Grand 67,115
- Petit 70,116
Cerise, Col de 84
Cessole, Cima di 96
Chafrion, Cime 59
Chaminèye(s), Cime(Mt.) 48
- Pas du 27,48
Chiotàs barrage 32
Cinq Lacs, Baisse des 72,73
Clapeirette, Cime de 73
Clapier, Mt. 50
- Pas E du (Mt.) 50
- Pas W du (Mt.) 50,53
Colomb, Brèche 65
- Cayre 64,110
- Gias 28
- Mt. 64
- Pas du Mt. 26,66
Conques, Pas des 45
Corno Stella 138
Costi biv. hut 33
Cougourde, Baisse de 75,77
- Cayres de 77,120
- hut 30
Cresta Savoia 132
Culatta, Colle della 95
Cuneo 19,24

Detriti, Pso. dei 98
Diable, Cime du 44
- Pas du 42
Dragonet peaks 33

Eboulis, Collet d' 97,98
Entracque 19,20,24
Erps, Cayre des 34,83,125

146

Fenestre, Cime E de 63
- Cime W de 63
- Col de 29,30,63
- valley 29
Ferisson, Baisse de 73
Fontanalbe valley 37,38,42
Font Frèye, Cime de 73
Forchetta, Colletto della 96,98
Fous, Pas de la 27,49
Fremamorte, Cime de 85
- Col de 85
Freshfield, Colletto 102

Gaisses, Cime des 75
Gandolfo biv. hut 33
Gélas, Balcon du 59,60,61
- Cime du 59
Gelas di Lourousa 100,136
Genova, Cima 102
- hut 32
Ghigo, Pta. 144
Giegn, Pte. 92,129
Gordolasque valley 25
Guides' chain 141
Guiglia biv. hut 36
Guilié, Cime 82
- Col (de) 34,83

Innomée, Pta. 144
Isola 2000 12,13

Ladres, Pas des 29,75
Lago Bianco hut 28
Lapasse, Mt. 73
Lombard, Cime du 75
Long, Pas du Lac 54,55
Lourousa couloir 105
- valley 33
Lup, Forcella del 144
Lusière, Cime 27

Madone, Cayre de la 67,115
Madone de Fenestre (hut) 19,29
Madre di Dio 96,134
Malaribe, Cime de la 79

Maledie, Cime de la 54,110
- Pas de la 55
- Pas NW de la 58
Manzone, Cresta 53
Margiole, Brèche 90
- Tête 92
Marre, Tête de 74
Matto, Mte. 105
Maubert, Cima 96
Mercantour, Cime du 83
- Col du 83
Mercière, Col 13
Meris valley 106
Merveilles hut 37
- valley 26,38,42
Mesches, les 37
Minière valley 37
Mollières les Adus 12
Moncalieri hut 28
Montolivo, Baisse 49
Morelli hut 33
Muffié, Cime de 45,46
Muraion, Caire 58
- Colletto del 58
- Pso. sop. del 28

Nasta, Cima di 95,134
- Colle di 96,99,100
Nègre, Aigs. du Lac 89,91
Neiglier, Mt. 70,119
- Pas du 73
Nice 18,19,23
- hut 25
Niré, Cime 48

Paganini, Cima 96
Pagari hut 28
- Pas de 53
- Serre de 55
- Sommet de 53
Palu, Cime de la 24,74
Paranove, Cime de 73
Peirabroc 53
Peirastrèche chalet 73

Pelago, Cayres Nègres du 83
- Mt. 83
Peyrebroc, Cime de 53
Piacenza, Pta. 143
Piagu, Cime de 24
Plan du Var 23
Plent, Pta. 143
Pollini, Cime 43
Ponset, Baisse du 70
- Brèche du 113
- Mt. 66,113
Pounchu, Cayre 86
Prals, Cime de la Vallette 73
- Col de 30,73
Préfouns, Cayre du 89,129
- Pas du 89

Questa hut 36

Remondino hut 33
Risso, Roche 64
Rogué, Cayre de 85
- Cime de 85
Rond, Mt. 58
Roquebillière 19,23
Rovina valley 32
Ruine, Col de la 80
- Tête de la 81

S. Anna di Valdieri 20
S. Giacomo 28,29
St. Dalmas-de-Tende 24,37
St. Grat 25,30

St. Martin-Vésubie 19,23
St. Robert, Cime 61
- Collet 61,63
- Pas du 62
Salèse, Cime de Pagari de 85
- Col de 32,85
- valley 32
Savoia, Cresta 132
Sestrières 12
Siula huts 29
Soria hut 29
Stella, Mte. 100

Tablasses, Pas des 87
- Tête des 86,129
Tende, Col de 24
Terme di Valdieri 20,24
Terrace, Col de la 58,60
Trem, Pas du 44
Turini, Col de 42

Valasco valley 36
Valdeblore 108
Valdieri 24
Valletta valley 33,36
Valmasque, Baisse de 26,27,44
- hut 38
- valley 37,38
Valmiana, Colle di 106
Varrone biv. hut 33
Veillos, Col de 108
Viglino, Cime 28,50